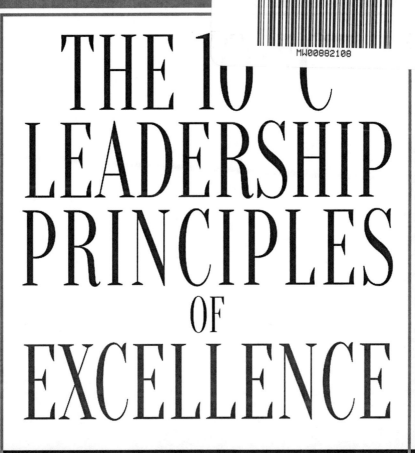

THE 10 C LEADERSHIP PRINCIPLES
OF
EXCELLENCE

WORKING TOWARD
THE BENEFIT OF THE TEAM

JEFF SCARPIELLO

outskirts
press

Table of Contents

Introduction i

1. Why the Hell Should I Write a Book? 1

2. Who Am I? 5

3. Principle 1 - Great Leaders Recognize Their Calling 14

4. Principle 2 - Great Leaders Exhibit Compassion 22

5. Principle 3 - Great Leaders
    Share the Culture of the Organization 31

6. Principle 4 - Great Leaders Exhibit Physical & Moral Courage ... 42

7. Principle 5 - Great Leaders Think Creatively 50

8. Principle 6 - Great Leaders Communicate Effectively 54

9. Principle 7 - Great Leaders Are Agents of Change 64

10. Principle 8 - Great Leaders Exhibit Confidence 70

11. Principle 9 - Great Leaders Are Capable 75

12. Principle 10 - Great Leaders Show Character 81

Final Chapter 87

Acknowledgements 90

References 92

About the Author 93

Introduction

This book is not a textbook; I've designed it to share with you some personal stories of what I have learned about leadership along my life's journey—both good and bad—that are filled with meaning, truth, and insight.

Whenever I talk with people in professional and social settings, I have learned of their desire to work for leaders who embody the characteristics that are most important to them. Unfortunately, like many of the people I've worked with in my career, it has been challenging to find the type of leader who meets the ideals I have found most important. My desire is to bring awareness to important leadership principles and to share them with others and that is what led me to write this book.

Leaders provide vision, inspire others to take action, and motivate others to believe they can accomplish anything. If you desire to be a leader in all areas of your life, *The Ten "C" Leadership Principles of Excellence* provide pillars to empower people and motivate them to keep focused on ten essential characteristics that are common among most great leaders: 1) Great Leaders Recognize Their Calling to Something Greater Than Themselves, 2) Great Leaders Exhibit Compassion, 3) Great Leaders Share the Culture of the Organization, 4) Great Leaders Exhibit Physical & Moral Courage, 5) Great Leaders Think Creatively, 6) Great Leaders Communicate Effectively, 7) Great

Leaders Are Agents of Change, 8) Great Leaders Exhibit Confidence, 9) Great Leaders Are Capable, and 10) Great Leaders Show Character.

As you journey through *The Ten "C" Leadership Principles*, my hope is that something that I've written will resonate with you on the essence of leadership—my desire is that each principle will motivate you to become more people-centered and focused on improving your life, both inside and outside of the workplace.

Are you ready to begin? Good, keep an open mind, and let's do it… *swoosh*!

CHAPTER 1

Why the Hell Should I Write a Book?

WHEN I CONTEMPLATED the idea of writing a book, my initial thoughts were that both of my kids are now in college, and I have way too much free time on my hands. I don't have too many hobbies besides spending time with my golden retriever, so I figured it would give me something productive to work on. I wondered, though, if I was motivated enough to actually begin the process of writing a book, much less finishing it. I also thought, would anyone care to read my thoughts about leadership?

Then it occurred to me that I'm a good storyteller—at least that's what my kids used to tell me when they were younger. What convinced me, though—no offense to any great thought leaders —was recalling the many leadership books I read throughout my master's in leadership degree program that bored the hell out of me. I realized, *"Hey, I have a master's degree in leadership and a unique background in government. I've attended well-known leadership programs and have been an Excellence in Government Fellow,"* so I decided to go for it. *"Yep,"* I told myself, *"just sit down and do it and see what happens."*

That's how I started—by just starting.

During the time I was in school, I questioned the value of a leadership degree versus getting a traditional MBA. I kept asking myself – *"Why did I let someone talk me into pursuing this program? What am I going to do with leadership degree?"* The next time I wanted more education, I'd have to marry a teacher, because this was it for me.

Well, I finally made it to graduation day—June 9, 2012, almost five years from the time I started the two-year degree program. The day that I graduated did not escape my attention - thirty years from the exact date I graduated from East Hartford High School, in Connecticut.

As I sat through the commencement ceremony, my ADD kicked into high gear and I found myself struggling to focus on the ceremony. I was scanning the crowd, chewing gum, half-assed listening and I was more concerned about where I was going to eat once the ceremony was over. As one featured speaker finished, I thought, *Great, I'm almost finished. Only two hours to go. Sigh.*

I glanced at the commencement program and saw that the next speaker was the new president of Nova Southeastern University, President Dr. George Hansbury. He was an older, distinguished, white-haired gentleman. As he began his speech I knew he'd better keep it short. I had to pee and the only thing keeping me from walking across the stage to get my diploma at this point, and go to the bathroom, was him. Even though my actual diploma had been mailed to me a few months earlier, I believed it was important for me to walk across the stage to let my teenage children see their old man get his degree. For five years, my family had heard me whine, complain and drop F bombs every time I had to complete an assignment. I think they were all as equally excited that I finished the course, just so I wouldn't be so grumpy any longer. Now if they wanted to pass me up academically, it would take a Ph.D. to do it.

Dr. Hansbury's speech caught me off-guard. Once he finished his laudatory welcoming remarks, he began to talk about the importance of things that were not necessarily associated with having earned a degree: such as giving back to others, ethics, honesty, integrity, making a difference in people's lives through good works, having character, and being pillars of the community. Only then did it hit me. *Shit, he was talking about what I just spent five years learning and about things that I thought were necessary attributes for life.*

As he continued I perked up in my chair. Now, here I was, at the pinnacle of my academic career, hearing words that I thought were more important than anything in the workplace. The importance of effective leadership was finally being recognized as equal, if not more important, than just having an academic degree.

Typically, when I look back on the many leaders I had worked with over the years, I seemed to remember them for all the wrong reasons. I felt many of them didn't understand leadership and became leaders by virtue of their title. In fact, even if I waved my magic leadership wand and tapped them on the head with it, they would still be clueless.

As I worked to develop a theme for my book–something that I thought would be worth sharing about my views on leadership–I recalled sitting through a speech by Mr. William Schoenhard, VA's deputy under-secretary for health for operations and management, speech to my leadership VA class.

Mr. Schoenhard was a soft-spoken, unassuming man, and quite frankly, one of the least likely people I ever thought would inspire me. Boy, was I wrong. His speech blew me away, and I really learned the axiom of not judging a book by its cover. It seemed like most of the topics he discussed started with the letter C, so I thought, *Okay, let's write a leadership book starting with character traits that begin with the letter C.* It was an odd concept to be sure, but it made sense to me because I always tell people that I believe compassion is what makes a person stand out most above all other character traits. So, I built off of the idea by writing a book based on the letter C, and, thus, *The Ten "C" Leadership Principles of Excellence* was born.

CHAPTER 2

Who Am I?

"WHO AM I" is a great song by the Christian pop-rock group - Casting Crowns. The song is inspired by Psalms 52 and 139 and Ephesians 2. The music speaks about God being there for us, believing in, and loving us, even though we seem unimportant in the grand scheme of life.

I have a rock on my desk with the words to the song written on it, so every time I look at it, I am reminded to focus on the core of who I am, my faith, and what I stand for and believe in--all important things great leaders should learn and know about themselves.

As a first-time author, I think it is also important for my readers to know who I am—my background—which helped framed my ideas on leadership. I wanted to freely share a brief narrative of some of the experiences that have shaped my life. These experiences, combined with my many years of leadership, in a variety of settings, inspired me to move forward and write this book.

I grew up in a single-parent household with three siblings and a mother who had a hard time trying to provide us the essentials for living. I am not ashamed to say that had it not been for government food and assistance programs, we would not have survived. I believe in the government providing a helping hand to people, not lifetime handouts—big difference. By the time I was eighteen years old, we had moved approximately fifteen times.

From a young age, I saw friends and family members do what they could to help our family, and that made a lasting impression on my life. My mother was both parents to me, as my father was constantly in and out of prison, hooking-up with women -- other than my mother, and an alcoholic to boot. It led me to my own truth, that it was almost more difficult for me to know that I had a father who wanted nothing to do with me than if he had died and I'd never known him. Not having a father or trying to do everything opposite of what he did has been the impetus for me to succeed throughout my life.

So, in all honesty, the first great leader in my life has been my Mom, Gloria Christiana—one of the greatest optimists I have ever met despite the very hard life she endured. She epitomizes the attributes that great leaders possess. She is unassuming and selfless, qualities from which respect is built. A prime example of this was when my mother brought a total stranger, a homeless woman off the streets of Los Angeles, into our home to live with us for almost twenty years prior to her death. When Katherine passed away, she did so with dignity, knowing she was loved and cared for by a family that loved her. My mother restored her honor and dignity, and that lesson is still etched in my memory.

My mom's actions remind me of a quote from Mother Theresa, "At the end of life we will not be judged by how many diplomas we have received, how much money we have made, how many great things we have done. We will be judged by 'I was hungry, and you gave me something to eat. I was naked and you clothed me. I was homeless, and you took me in."

Another seminal moment in my life occurred when I was twelve years old and attended a YMCA camp known as Camp Fox on Catalina

Island – twenty-six miles across the sea. This singular event became a cornerstone of my life. I became a Christian and remember God telling me that I was put here to do something great. It was during this time that I met YMCA male counselors who took an interest in me in a personal way that I had not yet experienced in life, having grown up without a father or strong male presence in my life.

To commemorate this event, I was led up a mountaintop on Catalina Island overlooking the Pacific Ocean until we reached a certain point. Then, I was blindfolded and led into position, awaiting the removal of my blindfold. A blue rag was placed over my head and draped onto my shoulder–this blue rag symbolized the commitment I made to focus on God, Country, and becoming my best self.

I then looked down and noticed I was standing around a design of white rocks that were arranged into four well-known shapes: the traditional YMCA triangle (representing spirit, mind, and body); the square-to signify the four-square life of a Ragger (spiritual, mental, physical, and social); the circle representing the circle of friendship amongst Raggers; and the cross symbolizing the center of the Christian's life. We then cited the Ragger's creed:

> I would be true for there are those who trust me.
> I would be pure for there are those who care.
> I would be strong for there is much to suffer.
> I would be brave for there is much to dare.
> I would be friend to all the foe - the friendless.
> I would be giving and forget the gift.
> I would be humble for I know my weakness.
> I would look up - and laugh - and love - and lift.

For several years after I was presented with my first rag, I returned to Camp Fox as a staff member for the summer and on school weekends. At the end of each summer I would cry while I was on the boat looking back at the island. I realized later in life I wasn't crying because I missed the island, but rather the relationships I had forged and how they shaped my thinking and the way I wanted to live.

On Catalina Island, I felt closer to God and more secure as a young person. Back on the mainland, as a teenager it was all about survival, just trying to get through my adolescence. Throughout my school years, I was an average student and always took the easiest class subjects just so I could pass the class. I was terrified of taking any classes ending in the letters Y or A in fear that I could not pass any science or math subjects. Sadly, when I graduated from high school in 1982, the requirements weren't very tough compared to today's graduation requirements. As a result, even though I made it through school, it was an empty intellectual experience because I never challenged myself to see what I was really capable of doing.

After high school graduation, I was not equipped to attend college. So, one day on a whim I walked into an Air Force recruiting station where I met with a recruiter to check out my options for joining the military. The technical sergeant I met with was a grisly-looking, seasoned Air Force member whose stench of cigarette smoke bothered me. As we talked, I made a joke which he interpreted as smart-assed comment from an 18-year-old. He immediately stood up and told me to get the "'fuck' out of his office." No adult in my life had ever spoken to me in such a manner, so now he had my full attention. I learned a lesson right then and there that strength can be attractive and grab people's attention. He told me "to shut up, so that I might learn something that can change my life."

After we finished talking and completing some paperwork, he said, "I'll be at your house at 5:00 a.m., tomorrow, to take you to enlist in the U.S. Air Force."

I went home and told my mother what happened and said, "I'm

leaving tomorrow, I think I just joined the Air Force." I didn't realize the full extent of what I had done until almost six months later while on leave and at home waiting to get assigned to a base in England, I looked in the mirror one day and saw my flat-top haircut and asked, *"What the hell did I just do with my life?"*

While in the Air Force, I always thought of myself as inferior to others, because I wasn't as educated or smart as many of my peers. The primary reason I could do so well was that I just outworked others and took on any assignment or opportunity to shine that came my way. Hard work and perseverance paid off.

As time passed, I started to take more of an interest in my education. But what started to bother me was having to salute newly minted 21-22-year-old 1st lieutenants or "butter bars" as we called them. Making less money than these former frat house and sorority sisters didn't sit too well with me and provided me with the impetus I needed to move on to the next phase in my life.

As fate would have it, I medically retired in 1994 and relocated from San Angelo, Texas, to Tampa, Florida with my then girlfriend and future bride, Tammy. Two days after arriving in Tampa, I enrolled at Hillsborough Community College, and used my veteran's benefits to get a two-year college degree. This was a big deal at that time, especially since I considered myself not very intelligent. Frankly, I had to start in many remedial classes, and had it not been for my wife's tutoring, and a serious kick-ass calculator, I would never have passed any of my math or science classes (those ending in Y and A).

I think the value of higher education was not necessarily just about academics. For me, completing each course that ultimately led to getting my degree was validation that I could achieve something that only years earlier I did not think was possible. School gave me the confidence to know I was on par with my fellow students and soon

9

after starting my Master's program, I had students in PhD programs asking for my help. This is when I knew I had something to contribute that others might value. I also learned that education encourages imagination, creativity, a thirst for knowledge, and it gives you the confidence to accomplish things outside your comfort zone that you otherwise might not think you were capable of doing.

My first post-military job was working as a national service officer for a veteran's service organization known as the Disabled American Veterans. Little did I know at the time, working and advocating on behalf of veterans was to become my life purpose, my calling. I continued with this job for four years, before, out of the blue, I got a call that changed my life.

I was contacted by the office of Bill Nelson, a newly elected U.S. Senator from Florida, whose staff had heard of the work I was doing to help veterans. He wanted to interview me to work for him. I was asked to drive to Winter Park, Florida, just outside of Orlando, for a 6:00 p.m. interview. It was already 2:00 p.m., and I was at my job unshaven and wearing a Mickey Mouse tie that day, so I hurried home, got cleaned up, and headed off to the interview.

What I didn't realize, was that I had mistaken Winter Park, FL for Winter Haven, FL which was very close to my home, so I left on the assumption that I had plenty of time to make it to my interview. At some point, I realized where I was supposed to go. As I made my way to Winter Park, it was heavily pouring rain and I was stuck on two-lane highway near Disney World along Interstate-4. There was bumper-to-bumper traffic with new construction everywhere. I was stuck in traffic for two hours experiencing serious road rage, and I didn't own a cell phone at the time. I just wanted to cry, turn around, and go home with the thought of seeing this wonderful opportunity slip through my fingers. But quitting is not in my nature, so I continued. I finally arrived at the interview location two hours late at 8:00

p.m. When I got there, the office door was locked, and there wasn't a single light on in the place. I rang the buzzer and couldn't believe someone was still there to let me in.

I ended up having the most extensive interview of my life that lasted until midnight. One interesting part of the interview required me to solve the following word puzzle: A man walks into a room, turns the radio on, walks upstairs, turns the lights on, walks over to the window, looks outside the window, opens the window, and jumps. The interviewer asks me to tell him what happened and why. I thought, *Shit, what are you talking about, dude?* He told me that I had thirty minutes to try to solve the problem and that he could only respond to my questions with yes or no answers. Very helpful, not!

I took off my jacket, loosened my tie, rolled up my sleeves, and went to work. I found out later this had impressed the interviewer who later ended up becoming a friend. I can proudly say I was able to solve the puzzle with two minutes to spare and later learned that it was not actually that important to solve the riddle. The point was to see my deductive reasoning skills, and most importantly, to see that I would not give up. I later found out that if a person gave up before the thirty minutes elapsed, they did not get the job. Oh, as for the riddle, I'll keep you curious, so you'll have to figure out the answer for yourself. If there's a second book within me, I'll include the answer.

An interesting tidbit is that the person who interviewed me served as one the models for the Vietnam War Memorial: Three Servicemen statue in Washington, D.C. One day in DC, I called him while looking at the statute and told him that a bird had just shit on his shoulder, his response was *"Be a pal and wipe it off for me"*. This gentleman, Jim Connell offered me the job right on the spot because he "liked my tenacity." He gave me a salary range and, not wanting to seem greedy; I asked for one dollar less than the maximum. He laughed, told me that was a great response, and gave me the full amount. When I asked him how they had gotten my name to interview, he told me that I had helped a friend of his and that person had given me a glowing recommendation. So when people ask me how I got to work for a U.S. Senator, I tell them I was nice to someone, and that person remembered me for it—no political nepotism or connections required.

Working for a U.S. Senator was exciting, interesting, challenging, rewarding, and to this day the best job I have ever had. I cried like a baby the day I left. The work gave me a wonderful sense of purpose, but literally almost killed me. I was taken by ambulance to the hospital one day with what I thought was a heart attack.

I knew it was time to resign, move on, make a better living for my family—and see my kids grow up minus the stress. What made the job so memorable, besides the crazy constituent stories I could tell, and will hopefully write about one day, was the colleagues I worked with. We all worked our asses off each and every day. When I hear people talk about how dissatisfied they are with government employees, how much money they make (*not!*), and the benefits they receive, I think to myself, *if they only knew the bullshit we had to put up with…well, they would not believe it.*

I describe my experience of working for a U.S. Senator as having three P's: power, perks and little pay. The P I enjoyed the most was possessing the power of the mythical Norse god of thunder - Thor! I was working for a U.S. Senator using an ethereal hammer to make huge differences in many people's lives by intervening on their behalf in numerous federal matters. You can accomplish great things if you wield power responsibly and know how to use it effectively.

Each year, I had the highest case workload in the office and most likely in the state of Florida. During my time in the senate, 9/11 occurred and I saw the greatness of this country as patriots from all eras who had already honorably served in the armed forces wanted to go back on active duty to protect their country once again. I saw fear as young Floridians were called to active duty and the horror when soldiers' families were notified of their deaths. I visited VA hospitals and saw the horrific wounds our soldiers had suffered. These wounds also impacted their loved ones who would have to care of them for the rest of their lives. I recall speaking with the mother of the most critically wounded soldier of the war at one point, and she referred to her son as her blessing despite the severity of his injuries. Hearing her say those words made me think there are consequences when our nation's leaders make decisions.

After leaving the U.S. Senate in 2008, I went to work at VA Central Office where I worked on Veterans' healthcare legislation, most notably to provide a series of new and enhanced services supporting family caregivers of the seriously ill and injured veterans. In May 2010, President Obama signed the Caregivers and Veterans Omnibus Health Services Act of 2010 authorizing the VA to establish a wide range of new services to support certain caregivers of eligible post-9/11 veterans. During my stint at the VA, I also played an integral role in starting a new organization dedicated to improving medical disability examinations in support of Veterans' claims for benefits.

After twenty-five years of combined public and legislative service, I decided to take a job in the private sector because I mistakenly thought my contentment was inextricably linked to making more money. Little did I know, as Luke 12:34 states, "For where your treasure is, there your heart will be also." Boy, was I wrong, there is so much more to life than money. It might be satisfying to have enough money to be able to rent happiness for a while, but it will not lead to your fulfillment.

CHAPTER 3

Principle 1 - Great Leaders Recognize Their Calling
(To Something Greater Than Themselves)

> *"We shall never learn to feel and respect our real calling and destiny, unless we have taught ourselves to consider everything as moonshine, compared with the education of the heart."*
>
> —Sir Walter Scott (1771-1832),
> British author of historical novels and ballads

AT MANY POINTS in my career, I've felt hopeless and unhappy. I would frequently come home miserable constantly complaining about how horrible my life was to my wife and small children. You know the saying, when Daddy's not happy, no one's happy; well, try living with someone like that for a while and it brings everyone down. One day, I was riding home with my then 10-year-old son, Jeffrey, being grumpy and talking about how much I hated life, my job, and just everything in general. I told him that I should have been promoted and should have been making much more money at that point in my life.

He turned to me and calmly stated, "Dad, did you ever think you are right where you are supposed to be in life and that helping me and

Lexy (his sister) grow up is what you are supposed to be doing? Then we can do something great."

Out of the mouth of a ten-year-old—he was perceptive and spoke the truth. He knew one of my calling's, my purpose in life, before I did!

Sometimes our purpose finds us when we least expect it. One prime example of this was a heart-wrenching story I saw on ABC, a special edition of 20/20. Diane Sawyer interviewed Sue Klebold, the mother of Columbine killer, Dylan Klebold. Even after seventeen years following the Columbine shooting, Ms. Klebold said, "it's very hard to live with the fact that someone you loved and raised has brutally killed people. I just remember sitting there and reading about them, all these kids and the teacher."

You could see the visible pain and anguish she continued to live with, as did the families of her son's victims. In an essay with *O Magazine* entitled "I Will Never Know," Ms. Klebold recounts how she was widely seen as an accomplice because the person she raised was considered a "monster." In one newspaper survey, 83% of the respondents said it was the parents' failure to teach proper values that played a major part in the Columbine killings. Ms. Klebold has now dedicated her life to helping other families recognize the warning signs of children living with mental illness. She has released a new memoir, *A Mother's Reckoning: Living in the Aftermath of Tragedy*. The profits will go toward research and charitable foundations focusing on mental health issues.

Other well-known great leaders like Abraham Lincoln, Mahatma Gandhi, Florence Nightingale, and Mother Theresa evidenced their passion by serving others. They led with their vision and ideas and brought them to fruition. They did not seek credit for a job well done, but instead got their satisfaction in helping to improve the lives of others through their deeds.

When I medically retired from the United States Air Force in 1994, I had no idea what I was going to do with my life. After eleven years of military service —after all I had ever done in my adult life was be in the military, I went through a period of uncertainty regarding where and what I was going to do next?

After separating from the military, I relocated to Tampa, Florida. I wanted to access my VA benefits and mistakenly called the Disabled American Veterans (DAV) for assistance to file a claim for disability benefits with the Department of Veterans Affairs. This subtle twist in my life reminds me of the poem by Robert Frost, *The Road Not Taken*. "I took the road less traveled by, and that has made all the difference."

While reaching out to DAV, I eventually ended up meeting with a gentleman named, Joe. He was elderly, around eighty years old; who worked as DAV voluntary chapter service officer. Quite frankly when I first met him, I thought he was a mangy-looking dude. He reminded me of the character Scar from the Lion King. He barely had any teeth, was disheveled and smelled awful. Not a very kind recollection. But, now that I am older and more mature, I realize this gentleman, a survivor of WWII, was a great leader who had found a purpose in life bigger than himself by giving back to help disabled veterans. He didn't receive a penny for his efforts, not recognition or any awards, but he was compelled to help others---end of story. His life's purpose was beyond himself.

Several years later, in a twist of fate, I became a national service officer for the Disabled American Veterans and was able to help him with a claim he filed only months before his death. The day we received word that his claim was approved was one of the greatest feelings I have experienced, because it was reminder that often in life, things come full circle, and that what you give to others comes back to you. The real gift is not in receiving something, but in giving to others. It can be infinitely more rewarding.

One thing I have learned about people is that everyone has a story to tell, and it generally revolves around something that they are passionate about. Some stories I've heard, especially from The Greatest Generation, as Tom Brokaw calls them—have been incredible. I have spoken with Former Prisoners of War, Medal of Honor recipients, Rosie the Riveters, a man who knew Albert Einstein, and plain ordinary folks from many walks of life that had such fulfilling lives. As we raise our own children, sometimes, we are so busy—at least in our own minds—that we don't take the time to listen and take in what we have heard. We only seem to talk about ourselves and what is important in our own lives. If we could all learn to listen without thinking about how to respond, we would truly understand each other better.

In 2012-2013, I was one of only ten Veterans Health Administration employees selected into the Partnership for Public Service Excellence in Government (EIG) fellowship program. The EIG program, as implied, "prepares leaders to be more than managers. They are innovators whose creativity in problem-solving stands up to the complexity of our 21st-century challenges. Our graduates deliver results—helping the government effectively defend the homeland, ensure public safety, protect the environment, respond to natural and man-made disasters, improve public health, and serve those in need."

Approximately one month before my EIG graduation, our class was required to read a *Fast Company* article by Alan M. Webber entitled "Are You Deciding On Purpose," an extended interview with Richard Leider. *Fast Company* noted that what has distinguished Leider throughout his three decades as a career coach and counselor is the philosophy he brings to difficult decisions about work and life. At the heart of his approach to counseling is a belief that each individual is born with a reason for being and that life is a quest to discover that purpose.

Fast Company spoke with Richard Leider about his "laws" for making decisions on purpose. The final interview question and answer caught my attention. Leider said that we should make decisions the way senior citizens wish they had. He stated the following:

> For nearly 25 years, I've been doing interviews with senior citizens, asking them to look back over their lives and talk about what they've learned. I've conducted more than 1,000 interviews with people who were successful in their jobs, who retired from leading companies after distinguished careers. Almost without exception, when these older people look back, they say the same things-things that are instructive and useful for the rest of us as we make decisions going forward in our lives. First, they say that if they could live their lives over again, they would be more reflective. They got so caught up in the doing, they say, that they often lost sight of the meaning. Usually, it took a crisis for them to look at their lives in perspective and try to re-establish the context. Looking back, they wish they had stopped at regular intervals to look at the big picture They also sounded a warning: Life picks up speed. The first half of your life is about getting prepared and getting established. Then time shifts gears. You hit the second half of your life, and everything moves faster.

Days turn into weeks, weeks into
months, and suddenly, you're 65
years old. Looking back, they say, you
realize that time is the most precious
currency in life. And as they got older,
having time for reflection became
even more important.
Second, if they could live their lives
over again, they would take more
risks. In relationships, they would
have been more courageous. And in
expressing their creative side, they
would have taken more chances. I
think it was Oliver Wendell Holmes
who said, "Most of us go to our
graves with our music still inside us."
Many of these people felt that, despite
their successes, their music was
still inside them. Almost all of them
said that they felt most alive when
they took risks. Just being busy from
business made them numb. Aliveness
came with learning, growing,
stretching, exploring.
Third, if they could live their lives
over again, they would understand
what really gave them fulfillment. I
call that the power of purpose: doing
something that contributes to life,
adding value to life beyond yourself.
Purpose is always outside yourself,
beyond your ego or your financial
self-interest.
We all want both success and

fulfillment. Success is often measured
in external ways, but there's an
internal measure of success, and it's
called fulfillment. Fulfillment comes
from realizing your talents-adding
value and living by your values.
Fulfillment comes from integrity, from
being who you are and expressing
who you are as fully as possible.
It doesn't have to do with your job
description or the specifics of your
work. It has to do with how you bring
yourself to your work, regardless of
what that work is.

This article had a powerful influence on my life because, by all objective measures, I think I was fairly successful—not so much in material ways, but in my ability to help others through a life of public service. However, this memory I have always kept of being twelve years old and having God tell me that I was put here to do something great has troubled me throughout my adult life.

What I learned through reading this article and about myself, was that I had already been doing something great in serving Veterans and that is what God had put me here to do. My calling was not a singular event, what I thought was needed to make a difference, but rather an accumulation of going to work each day trying to make a difference in the lives of others. This paradigm shift in thinking about trying to focus on the little things each day to help others is what has made a difference in helping me lead a more rewarding life.

Have you found your calling or purpose in life? If you have, congratulations! You are ahead of the game and a rare bird. If not, though, are your heartstrings tugging on you to do something you have felt in your soul for a long time? Don't wait any longer. As Steve Jobs once said, "Have the courage to follow your heart and intuition. They somehow already know what you truly want to become. Everything else is secondary."

Principle 2 - Great Leaders Exhibit Compassion

"No matter who we are, no matter how successful, no matter what our situation, compassion is something we all need to receive and give."
— Catherine Pulsifer, *Secrets of Success*

"One love, one heart, one destiny."
— Bob Marley, Legendary Jamaican Reggae Artist

EARLY IN MY career, I came across a talented entrepreneur who had all the requisite skills to become successful, and not surprisingly, he put his talents to work and founded a successful non-profit organization. However, in our private moments, I found he was critical and judgmental of others. Sometimes he would play it off, but even when he joked, he enjoyed taking cheap shots at other people's expense.

I recall a discussion we had that centered on the debate about whether someone who smoked marijuana in the military should receive a dishonorable discharge. This person was adamant that rules should never be broken and believed that whoever broke them deserved such a harsh punishment. I tried to explain that once a person has a dishonorable discharge it will negatively impact their ability through-out life to obtain employment and provide for their families and that every young person in life makes mistakes. He would have none of it. Finally, I turned to him and said,

"You know what makes a leader great?"

He said, *"What?"*

"Compassion," I replied, before walking away.

Most great leaders exhibit compassion and concern for others, some-times even when it is difficult to do. Let me give you an example of a choice I faced that could have destroyed someone's life and pos-sibly his family members' lives too and how/why I chose the route of compassion.

I accepted an assignment in Nashville, Tennessee and shortly after getting there was told by a senior executive to shut down an entire organization. He told me in short, that the employees were dysfunc-tional and the program not worth saving. It was a depressing situation, as I had to sit down with someone from human resources and call in roughly thirty employees to let them know we were closing the of-fice and that they did not fit into future plans. Have you ever seen the movie *Up in the Air* with George Clooney? In the movie, he travels from city to city to fire employees. I'm obviously no George Clooney, but I had to do the same thing. I knew that these individuals would not choose to relocate and that my life was about to get very ugly, quickly once I broke the news. For starters, we had to place a security guard outside the office in case things got out of control.

One of the first people I spoke with yelled, "This is outrageous!" and many thought it was a conspiracy that I was in on from the mo-ment I arrived in Nashville. The worst, though, was a man who put a silhouette shooting target in my office and verbalized to my secretary his intentions to physically hurt me.

Because I felt I was in danger; I immediately closed the office down for a couple of days and told all the other employees that we were having air conditioning problems. I had all the locks and door codes changed and revoked all of this individual's computer rights. The gentleman who threatened me was visited by police, questioned, and told not to return to work. Those in senior leadership positions in Washington D.C. washed their hands of the situation and told me it was my decision to make: begin the process of firing him from the federal government, or to do whatever it was I felt necessary, including pressing charges against him.

This was, without a doubt, a decision that weighed heavily on my heart. I knew that if I fired him, it would ruin his life and ability to provide for his family. I felt horrible that all these employees were being let go and could understand why this person was so threatening and desperate that he would want to hurt me—the messenger of this decision.

When I met with this individual to discuss his future, I told him that no one in upper management cared about the situation, or quite frankly him, and had left it up to me to decide his fate. I told him I decided not to press charges. Further, that he would have to work from home and attend anger management counseling and once that was completed, I would evaluate the situation and make a final decision on whether to terminate his employment.

This gentleman literally broke down crying, thanking me for, as he put it, "not ruining his life." In retrospect, I think I made the right decision because this person is once again a productive employee for another organization.

Another great leadership lesson I learned out of this situation is that real leaders aren't cowards; they must do the unpleasant stuff themselves if they want to have any credibility. This is a hard lesson for many, but I think it is important for leaders to be able to distinguish the person from the act.

How do you exhibit acts of compassion both at work and in your personal life? Are you a compassionate leader?

- ***Great leaders exhibit their greatest strengths and/or weaknesses by how they act and treat others.***

According to Google spokesman, Jordan Newman, Google's various offices and campuses around the globe reflect the company's overarching philosophy, which is nothing less than "to create the happiest, most productive workplace in the world."

Google's leadership gets it. They know how to have fun and make the workplace fun for others. Newman said, "They push the boundaries to let its hundreds of software engineers, the core of its intellectual capital, design their own desks or workstations out of what resembles oversized Tinker Toys."

As Newman states, "Some have standing desks, a few even have attached treadmills so they can walk while working. Employees express themselves by scribbling on walls. The result looks a little chaotic, like some kind of high-tech refugee camp, but Google says that's how the engineers like it."

Good leaders work hard but understand the value of sharing smiles with others all while getting the job done. Even when they are stressed with time constraints and difficult projects, they show encouragement to others and don't let how they are feeling change their behavior, because no one wants to work with prickly bosses or, for that matter, co-workers. Great leaders approach each day with a positive attitude/spirit and stay loose. They understand the importance of the work/life balance and do not live to work, but rather work to live so that life is not boring. They enjoy family time and friends as well, and make time for everyone, including you.

The adage: "if you want respect, show respect" is accomplished by acting in ways that show you recognize your colleagues as people who deserve respect. As such, you recognize that they have rights, opinions, wishes, experience, and competence. You understand that these people are worthy of additional responsibilities, more meaningful work, and recognition regardless of their titles or positions, but based upon the performance, values, qualities, and capabilities that they bring to the workplace.

Individuals who prove they are responsible leaders gain the respect and trust of their followers. Employees who do not respect you are likely to ignore you and become unresponsive unless it suits their own purposes. Leaders who show respect to others undoubtedly will inspire admiration in others.

- *Great leaders show empathy by understanding others' personal and professional challenges.*

Many managers are content with wielding power and authority, often at the expense of genuinely caring for others.

Converting power to influence first requires a leader to lead by example. It has been said many times that the only moral guideline people will follow is the example set by their leaders. The second thing a leader must do is show the requisite empathy toward his/her employees. People want to feel like leaders' care (while respecting their positions of authority) about their well-being. True leaders understand that employees want to be treated the way a leader wants to be treated. These two concepts are necessary to preserve the leader/ employee relationship dynamic.

Leaders who show an interest in their employees beyond the mundane day-to-day activities are essential in an organization. They don't choose to talk to people selectively. They understand that you never know who or when someone will be needed to step up in key situations.

A former female employee, not overly friendly, was always suspicious of management's motives. She seemed to enjoy questioning authority, always against the backdrop of filing some equal employment opportunity complaint. One early morning, she stood outside my office. I could sense something was not right because she rarely spoke with people outside of her peer group.

She entered my office and shared with me that as a single mother she was having problems raising one of her children. She started to bawl and told me she was on medication and that she could no longer function at work. She thought she was having a nervous breakdown. I could have told her, "I'm sorry to hear that, but that is not my problem." Instead, I empathized with her situation, consoled her, and guided her to some resources to try to help her. I encouraged her to take the time off she needed to get healthy and told her I did not judge her in her time of need—that it was okay to let go of her emotions.

Have you ever had a bad day at home or work and just needed someone to listen to you without judging? Good leaders make themselves available and provide comfort when needed to show their employees they care about them as people first, not employees—an important distinction.

- *The Platinum Rule: Treat others better than you want to be treated.*

Most everyone knows the Golden Rule, which has been attributed to Jesus of Nazareth who used it to summarize the Torah, "Do to others what you want them to do to you. This is the meaning of the law of Moses and the teaching of the prophets" (Matthew 7:12 NCV, see also Luke 6:31).

Taking it one step further, Dr. Tony Alessandra, a professor and prolific author who delivers college lectures in an entertaining fashion, says people should follow the Platinum Rule, which is to "Treat others the way they want to be treated." What a difference it makes to accommodate the feelings of others. It shifts the focus of relationships. Dr. Alessandra states, "This is what I want, so I'll give everyone the same thing to let me first understand what they want, and then I'll give it to them."

So, how do you determine how people want to be treated? Easy question, you ask them. You sit down and talk with them, find out what makes them tick, what their dreams, goals and aspirations are in the workplace and in life—anything that can help you gain insight into their world. If you can learn successfully to apply the "Platinum Rule," you'll greatly improve the quality and effectiveness of your interactions with others.

- *Great leaders make sure their actions match their words, and that they "walk the talk."*

Do you feel like you are being taken care of and respected by those within your organization? Sir Richard Branson of Virgin Atlantic, who decided to grant one year of paid paternal leave to his employees, clearly understood the importance of taking care of his people. He said in a public statement, "If you take care of your employees, they will take care of your business." Let me take it a step further. If you take care of people through a sense of loyalty, they will gladly go through a wall for you!

His statement is my modus operandi. Looking back on my most pleasant work experiences, the people who performed the best and who were the most productive, invariably felt well cared for—respected, rewarded, and secure. Conversely, when employees felt, for whatever reasons, that I didn't sufficiently "have their back," loyalty quickly waned. The attitude of one of my employees changed virtually overnight when she felt I wasn't doing enough to advocate forcefully for her during a period of uncertainty and organizational upheaval. In retrospect, I've come to believe she was right. Although she was a pain-in-the-ass, she took care of the business. The mistake was mine, and I paid a high price by losing her loyalty and confidence in the process.

Similarly, when I think back on myself as an employee (as most managers, of course, were also employees), I was motivated to perform best when I felt a manager had my interests at heart and genuinely tried to develop and help me advance personally and professionally. Also, when I sensed a manager lost focus on the mission and more focused on his or her advancement, there's no question I developed a disdain for working for them and led me to resent working for them and questioning their motivations.

J.W. Marriott often advised Marriott's managers by voicing a deeply held belief that remains the keystone of the company's culture that if you "Take care of associates, they'll take care of your customers." Remember, if they don't follow this maxim, you will likely not be able to change their behavior.

A great lesson I learned while in basic military training is the power of affirmation. I can recall like it was yesterday (now thirty-five years later) my drill instructor, Sergeant Williams, who weighed no more than 150 lbs., who wore his uniform impeccably, with his boots gleaming like glass. I recall Sergeant Williams once conducting a uniform and locker inspection standing right in front of me, like the scene that was played out by Louis Gossett Jr., and Richard Gere in the film *An Officer and a Gentlemen.* He approached me with his taps/heels-on clicking the floor, looking me up and down for what seemed like several minutes, when it was probably five-seven seconds. He stared intently at me from head-to-toe, looking for any flaws he could find. I knew if he found a demerit and pulled a piece of paper on me, my life would be hell for the next couple of days resulting in some form of punishment or corrective action. I thought to myself, *Shit, he's going to mess with me and I'm toast! He's going to ream me for whatever he wants!*

He looked me straight in the eye and said, "Airman Scarpiello, did you shine your boots with a Hershey bar?"

"No sir," I replied, as I heard the person next to me chuckle for a millisecond before stopping so he wouldn't get cursed at. The drill instructor then calmly and clearly said to me, "You represent the finest fighting force in the world, the U.S. Air Force; take pride in your uniform and yourself. You should always try your best and expect better from yourself and I know you will moving forward". He then walked away to inspect the next airman in formation.

To this day, these words have been a part of my ethos whatever or wherever I have worked or tried to accomplish. What was most impactful, is that Sergeant Williams did not use fear and intimidation to make me do something better. He exhibited a simple act of caring and compassion and it was evident to me that he meant what he said and walked the talk.

When I became an instructor almost eleven years later, I remembered his example and used it to guide me when working with recruits. I know that being a compassionate leader pays off, because I always received requests from my trainees to attend their graduations from technical training. I believe those invitations were their way of saying, "See, Sergeant Scarpiello, I learned something from you, and you made a difference in my life."

CHAPTER 5

Principle 3 - Great Leaders Share the Culture of the Organization

"Maintaining an effective culture is so important that it, in fact, trumps even strategy."
— *Howard Stevenson*

Everybody blames the culture without taking responsibility.
— *James Levine*

To merely observe your culture without contributing to it seems very close to existing as a ghost.
— *Chuck Palahniuk*

- **Great leaders strive to create a culture and atmosphere where employees appreciate each other's differences**

EMPLOYEES SHOULDN'T DREAD coming to work each day. In places where I've worked and the culture was strong most employees looked forward to going to their jobs and had a hard time leaving because they enjoy the challenges, their co-workers, and the atmosphere.

While the work may be difficult, the culture shouldn't add to the stress of the work. On the contrary, the culture should be designed to alleviate the work-related stress and even include some fun.

Creating a strong company culture allows us to work effectively with people from a variety of ethnic, cultural, political, religious, and socioeconomic backgrounds. It is being aware and respectful of the values, beliefs, traditions, and customs of those we serve while understanding that there is often a wide range of differences within and among groups. It is being aware of how our culture influences how we view others.

It's also important to know that you don't have to be the recognized leader in your workplace to help set the culture of the organization. I've had many employees take the lead in decorating the office, recognizing special occasions, bringing in cupcakes and just trying to make the workplace a more enjoyable place for all. My finest experience of working with someone who set the culture of the organization was a co-worker, Bruce Grimes. He was quite a bit older than everyone on the team, but no matter how rough the waters, or the chaos that would ensue due to the high stress associated with our job, he had a calming influence on everyone. He would have the presence of mind in the most difficult situations to stop me in my tracks, and remind me, "We can only do one thing at a time, and we need to do it right before we move on to the next thing."

He would wear a cheery bow tie each day and write poems, often including his co-workers in them. These seemingly small acts made a big difference on employee morale and help set the tone and culture for how others acted in the organization.

- **Great leaders utilize the talents of a diverse workforce integral for the long-term success of the organization.**

When I think of the word "team," the first thought that comes to mind is the adage that, "There is no 'I' in team." I also love the illustration that a single horse can pull a certain amount of weight alone, but when paired with another horse, the combined weight they can pull greatly increases beyond their individual capacity. This essence of team dynamics is this synergistic force that drives teams toward the completion of some goal. The act of placing team members in roles that maximize their skills plays an important role in achieving organizational effectiveness.

As I watched the Denver Broncos and Carolina Panthers play in Super Bowl 50, and Denver dominating on defense, I heard someone say, "It takes eleven players to make one offense." Isn't that the truth? No one player, no matter how good, can lead a team to victory. Sorry, Cam Newton. Even the greatest basketball player of all time, Michael Jordan, didn't win all those championships by himself. He played with two other Hall-of-Famers, Dennis Rodman and Scottie Pippen, and Jordan's other teammates played complementary roles to suit the team's needs.

Great leaders don't segregate different parts of the business so that employees don't know each other or how they collectively contribute to the overall good of the organization. Instead, they realize that each person is a link in a chain and that the organization is only as strong as the weakest link.

- **Great leaders make others feel valued and a productive part of a team regardless of position in the organization.**

Top-performing companies define their culture early. Have you heard of the phrase, "Treat the janitor as well as you would treat the CEO?" I keep seeing it posted all over the Internet, so it must be important, right? The reality is that it is not frequently practiced. Often, we look beyond the person and only see the titles associated with a name.

There is nothing worse than an employee who feels he or she is not an integral part of the organization. I once worked for an employer who went straight into the office and sat at his desk each day and had little interaction with his employees. The only thing he cared about each day as he stared at his computer monitor was whether his stocks were going up and down. This leader checked-out and his employees knew it. They had no respect for him and thus were always looking for their next job.

It is paramount to any organization that the culture and goals are explained to potential and current employees, and that they understand and acknowledge their responsibility to uphold the climate of the organization. If the value system of the organization tremendously contrasts from the value system of the employee, that employee is likely to look for other work that better complements his or her belief system.

The television hit show Undercover Boss is a great example of why leaders need to get out and spend time with employees. Frontline staff can often provide insights to the undercurrents of what is going on in an organization where it matters the most—away from the boardroom where the managerial work is done. In each episode, the leader of a company goes parading around different parts of the country in disguise, learning what goes on in his or her company by performing some of the same tasks that employees routinely accomplish. What these leaders always learn is that appreciation, inclusion, job security, and working for a sympathetic boss is equally, if not more important, than the wages employees received for their work. They also take away useful feedback from employees to improve operations. Almost without fail, the undercover boss learns that even though many employees have had to overcome personal and professional challenges they are highly motivated to do a good job. I don't think any employee comes to work each day thinking – how can I screw things up today.

I think servant leaders are the best at creating strong workplace cultures because they are interested in focusing on the needs of others, especially team members, before they consider their own needs. They acknowledge other people's perspectives, and give them the support they need to complete their work and personal goals, involve them in decisions when appropriate, and build a sense of community within their teams. This leads to higher engagement, more trust, and stronger relationships with team members and other stakeholders. It can also lead to increased innovation.

As leaders, we can start to build a sense of community within our organization's by focusing on the little things. Create opportunities for people to interact with one another in the company; provide and encourage social activities both inside and outside of the workplace.

One of my former bosses held staff meetings in the park outside the office right next to the beach. We used to have social functions at the dog track, recognize special events such as birthdays, have lunch with employees, host potluck lunches for which everyone would contribute something that the team would enjoy eating, and invite people to participate in a Christmas gift exchange.

The workplace was set up to allow others to communicate away from their desks. Each morning I would walk around and have casual conversations, getting to know my colleagues on much more than a business level. We would talk about our families, sharing stories about our children and with each other on a personal level. When we had conversations like this, I was more than just a boss to them, I was a genuine person who believed in and cared about them. This small act of reaching out and getting to know my colleagues allowed me to form strong bonds and open communication. Thus, many of them would do anything I asked of them because they trusted me. Many of these relationships remain in place today long after working together.

- ***Great leaders think about how to go above and beyond.***

Great leaders step outside their defined roles and do what they can to help. They are proactive. They don't wait to come up with ideas; they work to implement them. They stretch their thinking, they don't keep secrets from their employees, and they are engaged in the day-to-day activities.

Going above and beyond can be as simple as bringing in a box of donuts once in a while, publicly thanking employees, sending them private emails of encouragement, sharing words of wisdom, recognizing birthdays and work day anniversaries, and giving credit to people for a job well done. It never killed anyone to utter a kind word.

- ***Great leaders don't seek to get credit; they simply do the right thing.***

I worked with an individual who seemingly never choose to do the right thing without having an ulterior motive that benefited him. He always wanted credit for it. I once recall trying to help an organization feed the homeless and this person saying, "How will we get recognized for helping? "I responded, "Credit for what? Trying to help feed homeless people?" I truly believe that when you do the right thing, that is a reward in itself. Always try to be the giver of the gift and you will feel an internal joy, that will exceed the materialism of this world.

Contrast the person's attitude above with the following excerpt taken from a *Forbes* leadership article by John Baldoni on February 8, 2015 entitled, *Dean Smith: Coaching Us to Do the Right Thing*. "When you do something right, do not seek recognition for it."

That was the essence of a comment that Dean Smith made to John

Feinstein about not wanting to be remembered for helping to deseg-regate restaurants in Chapel Hill, North Carolina, 1958. Feinstein, an author and sportswriter for the *Washington Post*, had covered Smith for years and got to know the man personally.

Remembering Smith from NPR on his death, Feinstein noted how Smith entered a lunchroom with a black man who was a member of Smith's church. This was a risky move for a young coach in the seg-regated South, and years later, Smith's pastor related the incident to Feinstein. When Feinstein recalled the story to Smith, the coach was disappointed that his pastor had noted it. When Feinstein pressed Smith as to why he would not be proud of his actions as a young man, Smith replied, "John, you should never be proud of doing the right thing; you should just do the right thing!"

The Steve Harvey Show has a segment called "Harvey's Heroes." On one particular episode, Steve spoke with Mark Pizzo, a mailman who rescued a seven-year-old girl from the jaws of an attacking dog, ul-timately saving her life. As Mark was delivering mail, he noticed a young child being attacked by a dog. The dog literally had the young girl's braids in his mouth and was dragging her under a trampoline. Mark exited his truck and tried to get the dog to release the girl's head from his jaws. The dog would not release the child, so he ended up punching the dog in the head repeatedly until he released the girl. The dog then went on to attack a neighbor who had come over to try to help. The young girl was taken to the hospital where she had to have seven staples put into her head to stop the bleeding. Steve asked Mark if he felt he was a hero, and Mark said, "Some people say that, but I don't consider myself a hero, I'm just a guy that did the right thing."

Steve said, "No, you are a hero. Doing the right thing when most people wouldn't have gotten involved makes you a hero."

- *Great leaders relentlessly promote their beliefs with boundless energy.*

Great leaders do not have to state their beliefs loud, proud, and bold, or be politically incorrect. That is left to the demagogues. Great leaders exhibit passion, but these same individuals can also be quiet leaders who carry a big stick aka President Harry Truman. Employees are motivated and inspired to take action when they are convinced that the speaker is authentic and fights to promote what they believe.

As a subject matter expert on Veterans' issues, I have had the opportunity to give many speeches/presentations before crowds of Veterans, and typically I've had to speak after elected officials' remarks. These individuals are far more polished speakers than I am. My voice is hoarse and raspy at times, but I can't tell you how many times people in the audience have come up to me after I've spoken to tell me that my speech was moving, energetic, and heartfelt. They could tell I believed what I was saying, unlike the politicians who they said, "gave lip service" to the crowd. I'll take sincerity and substance over theatrics every time and so will most people

- *Great leaders' express confidence in their followers' ability and motivate them to achieve high standards.*

Great leaders understand how everyone contributes to the company's business and overall success and recognize everyone's role in completing the mosaic of the company—the big picture. They likewise understand brand awareness and how it will give employees inspiration and a sense of accomplishment.

It is important to know what motivates employees, because studies have shown, contrary to most beliefs, that money is not the sole motivating factor (Bolman & Deal, 2003). Employee behavior is linked to attitudes, and motivation helps employees achieve personal and organizational goals (Dickson, 1973). If motivation drives behavior, it is important to know then what motivates people. Is it money, job security, promotions, achievement, or something negative like the fear of failure?

Perhaps motivation simply changes over time as we progress through the various stages of our careers, and we either achieve or fail to meet specific goals. Personally, my intrinsic and extrinsic motivational factors have greatly changed as my career progressed. First, people need to understand there is a significant difference between a job and building a career. Now as a leader, the trick is to recognize the power of learning as to what drives individual behavior in the workplace.

Studies have shown that what tends to motivate employees to put forth their best efforts and to perform better at high levels are praise and recognition (Nelson, 2002). This fact is borne out from many careers in which individuals are grossly underpaid, yet enjoy the feeling of accomplishment in helping others. Once a person makes enough money to meet their monthly obligations, they strive to work in an environment where they can contribute to accomplishing meaningful work. It is important to recognize that motivation gives purpose and direction (Kreitner, 1995).

Why does someone go to great lengths to work late or put forth an extra effort? The answer seems simple but is often overlooked by leaders. People will respond when they receive praise and recognition for a job well done. I don't work hard because I make good money; that's what I'm paid to do. I am motivated because I don't want to let the team down. We trust each other and want to contribute to some meaningful success.

Have you ever noticed how the people who do all the right things are overlooked while others who scheme and are false are rewarded? Unfortunately, it is the organization that loses in the end, because the employees who care about fulfilling a particular vision are forced to find jobs that fulfill a need so much greater than money. I hope that by touching on this experience, you will understand how important it is for leadership to get to know their staff and understand what motivates them to work. Each employee is unique and requires different rewards and motivation.

Understanding what motivates employees can improve an employer's chance of retaining great talent. Employers sometimes make the mistake of paying an employee a high salary, believing it will guarantee high job performance. This is not necessarily the case. Employees want to feel that their work is worthwhile and that their salaries are commensurate with the work.

In a study of *Understanding Employee Motivation*, Lindner (2008) found that interesting work and good pay are keys to higher employee motivation. The ranked order of motivating factors was: interesting work, good wages, full appreciation of work done, job security, good working conditions, promotions and growth in the organization, feeling of being in on things, personal loyalty to employees, tactful discipline, and sympathetic help with personal problems.

What does this research mean? The research is a wake-up call to organizations that motivation for each person varies and can be difficult to predict, but guessing is not an option. If leaders want to learn what types of rewards motivate their employees, they will have to sit down with each employee and simply ask. When a leader takes the time to ask the right questions, the answers will show the organization what it needs to do to maximize effectiveness and productivity of its employees.

Carefully designed reward systems that include job responsibilities, job enrichment, promotions, internal and external stipends, monetary, and non-monetary compensation should be considered.

What motivates you to perform at your best? In turn, what can we do to motivate our employees to give their best every day?

CHAPTER 6

Principle 4 - Great Leaders Exhibit Physical & Moral Courage

"Integrity is telling myself the truth. And honesty is telling the truth to other people."
— Spencer Johnson, Motivational Author

"Real courage is doing the right thing when nobody's looking. Doing the unpopular thing because it's what you believe, and the heck with everybody."
— Justin Cronin, *The Summer Guest*

"If there is anything that links the human to the divine, it is the courage to stand by a principle when everybody else rejects it."
— Abraham Lincoln,
16th President of the United States

I BEGAN WRITING this chapter on Martin Luther King Jr. Day, 2016, which just goes to show that timing is everything since I had already decided I wanted to write about people who exhibited physical and moral courage. I think the story of how MLK lived his life epitomizes physical and moral courage because he didn't just fight for civil rights for African-Americans; he put his beliefs into action and his life in danger so that the future would be better for generations of all races and ethnicities to follow.

King, taking after Gandhi, showed moral courage through non-violence. He was a peaceful leader who used his words and actions to inspire a generation. He demonstrated moral courage by speaking on civil rights to the point of being insulted everywhere he went, spit on, beaten up, and even arrested numerous times, yet he never considered stopping before achieving his dream of seeing all humans treated equally. Ultimately, fighting for his dream cost him his life.

A recent Nobel Peace Prize recipient, the youngest in history, Malala Yousafzai, was a Pakistani schoolgirl who defied threats of the Taliban in order to campaign for the right to a girl's education. She survived being shot in the head by the Taliban. She now lives in the UK, and has become a global advocate for human rights, women's rights, and specifically, a girl's right to education.

Another person, not known by many, is Concepcion Picciotto, the protester who maintained a peace vigil outside the White House for more than three decades, a demonstration widely considered the longest-running act of political protest in U.S. history. She died on January 25, 2016, and was believed to be eighty.

Ms. Picciotto, a Spanish immigrant, known to many as "Connie" or "Conchita," was the primary guardian of the anti-nuclear-proliferation vigil stationed along Pennsylvania Avenue, the backside of the White House. In a 2013 profile in the *Washington Post*, Ms. Picciotto said she spent more than thirty years of her life outside the White House "to stop the world from being destroyed." By her presence, she said she hoped to remind others to take whatever action they could, however small, to help end wars and stop violence, particularly against children. Despite the perpetual tension, Ellen Thomas, a demonstrator, along with her husband, William, who protested with Ms. Picciotto, told the Post that the trio had protested together in the park for twenty-five years. The group's grass-roots nuclear disarmament campaign was known as "Proposition One," and its crowning achievement came in 1993 when a nuclear disarmament petition circulated by the activists resulted in a ballot initiative passed by district voters.

As the *Washington Post* noted, Eleanor Holmes Norton, the district's congressional delegate, helped the activists prepare a nuclear disarmament and conversion act, which she has since introduced in nearly a dozen sessions of Congress. The legislation has never reached the floor for a vote.

Do you have courage in your home and workplace to change things when you know they are wrong? What does your moral compass tell you? Can you imagine having the physical and moral courage to live in nothing but a small open tent, braving the elements for over thirty years for your beliefs? How will you stand up for your beliefs?

- *Great leaders show intensity for their beliefs.*

Vince Lombardi famously said this about intensity: "There's only one way to succeed in anything, and that is to give it everything. I do, and I demand that my players do."

Great leaders believe what they are saying and understand the motives that ignite human behavior. I am a die-hard sports fan, and the sporting world is filled with great examples of individuals showing the intensity of their beliefs. Although this football analogy may be a bit extreme, did you ever watch former All-Pro linebacker, Ray Lewis, of the Baltimore Ravens work his teammates into a frenzy before each game in the tunnel before they took the field? Did you think that Ray Lewis and the Ravens were going to lose any game after seeing how he fired up his teammates each week before the game? Hell no, I would be scared to play against them. They looked like rabid dogs getting ready to enter the gladiator's arena to battle to the death, even though it was only a simple football game. Ray Lewis, along with his teammates, visualized and dreamed of success with the core belief that the hours of training, practice, and personal sacrifice would yield results of spectacular catches, jaw-breaking hits, and ultimately, wins. Football players put their bodies on the line each week, and each week show the intensity of the beliefs with which they will play their game.

- ***Great leaders never give up or give in.***

Thomas Edison famously said, "Many of life's failures are people who did not realize how close they were to success when they gave up" He also stated that "our greatest weakness lies in giving up. The most certain way to succeed is always to try just one more time."

Former North Carolina State basketball coach Jim Valvano, who was dying of cancer got out of bed to attend the ESPY awards to receive the Arthur Ashe Courage Award. At that time, he delivered one of the most moving speeches I have ever heard. In fact, I watch the speech annually to remind myself of the importance of what he exhorted: "Don't give up, don't ever give up." Even when the odds are against you, when people doubt you or your ability to succeed, you can still achieve your goals. In fact, even after his death, Coach Valvano's V Foundation for Cancer Research has raised millions of dollars to find the cure for cancer. Coach Valvano believed, as many people do, that steel is forged in fire. This is the time when we must buckle down, stay the course, and be true to our core values.

As a famous four-star Army general, George S. Patton once said,

"Don't ever let up. Don't ever think that your job is unimportant. Every man has a job to do, and he must do it. Every man is a vital link in the great chain."

- ***Great leaders stand up and do the right thing under difficult circumstances***

Dr. Gerald M. Cross, the former acting under secretary for health for the United States Department of Veterans Affairs, and my former boss, was a great example of a humble leader who was willing to take the heat off other people for the good of the organization. I recall once while in the process of getting ready for a Congressional hearing before the Senate Committee on Veterans' Affairs, our written testimony that was required to be delivered three days before the committee hearing had not been delivered on time. Prior to the hearing, Dr. Cross was called in to speak with the committee chairman and was told he would not be given the opportunity to give his testimony. A refusal that a group not be allowed to give testimony before the committee was their way of trying to publicly embarrass the agency.

Dr. Cross sat through the opening statement from the committee chairman and ranking member and was eviscerated for the lateness of the testimony. The ranking member (minority party in Congress) kept prodding, trying to score political points, by badgering Dr. Cross to find out why the testimony was late. The ranking member was fishing, hoping to get a nice sound bite for his press release that he could use against the Administration. Dr. Cross could have easily thrown the White House Office of Management and Budget under the bus. It was their fault the testimony was late because they did not clear it on time. Instead, though, Dr. Cross calmly stated, "I am the witness and am responsible for the testimony, and; therefore, I am the one to blame for this testimony being late." The ranking member smiled and said something to the effect, "You are a good soldier, and we fully know the reason it was late, and it was not your fault." I don't know many men like Dr. Cross, who have the ethos that the buck stops with them.

- **Great leaders show moral courage and exhibit high ethical standards.**

Great leaders bring integrity to the job. Whether you are running the company or cleaning its restrooms, be honest in all you do. Don't call in sick just to get a day off—that's stealing. Put in an honest day's work for pay and hold yourself accountable as you would those around you. If you're working remotely, be sure you are doing what you are being paid to do. Always follow through and do what you have said you're going to do, because honesty, integrity, and reliability, mean everything to your employer and your reputation. Once you lose trust, it is hard to regain, if not impossible.

Making ethical decisions is the most fundamental characteristic of leadership. A leader's decisions will influence the culture and attitude of his or her co-workers and will permeate throughout the organization. Individuals who are quickly able to discern an ethical question may be more in tune to make more thoughtful decisions in accordance with their core beliefs (Butterfield, Trevino, & Weaver, 2000).

Leaders must always remain vigilant against compartmentalizing their core beliefs simply to justify their actions. During World War II, many of Hitler's henchmen spent the week sending Jewish prisoners to their death in the gas chamber and still found time to attend church on Sunday. For leaders, self-deception has significant moral implications. For instance, Reynolds (2005) cites Tenbrunsel's research noting that euphemisms often soften the blow of word choices. For example, words such as aggressive accounting practices (do whatever it takes to make the numbers work), collateral damage (civilians dead), downsizing (firing and laying off employees), leverage, maximizing, and rationalization, are all open to a great deal of interpretation that can lead to potentially unethical decision-making. Words help distance us from the reality of situations, and if we're not vigilant to even the slightest changes, we can deceive ourselves into making unethical decisions.

- *Great leaders model behavior for others by setting the example.*

As leaders, we should ask ourselves, *"Am I modeling what I want my employees and organization to become?"* Modeling behavior includes showing employees how to do a task, teaching them to perform specific skill sets, and having patience with them as they learn to master the skills successfully that should ultimately lead to increased workplace productivity. Rather than simply telling employees how to do the things they need to do or furnishing them with an instructional guide, take the time to perform the work yourself in front of them or pair them with experienced employees. Modeling behavior in this way allows employees to ask questions and gain insights from those with first-hand experience and helps them to take responsibility for their work; overall adding a greater sense of contribution to the success and objectives of the organization.

Never forget that employees pay attention to the non-verbal cues they observe. They watch and pay attention to the leaders' work ethic. Somehow, employees always know if their bosses are reading the newspaper and surfing the Internet when they should be working. They watch closely to see if the boss takes extended coffee and lunch breaks. They notice when the boss singles out other employees. Employees look at their watches to see if the boss is punctual in getting to work and whether he or she stays all day or works late to ensure the project is completed. Does the leader show that he or she is all-in with the employees when something has to be done and time is of the essence? A good modus operandi to practice and live by is never to ask anything of your employees that you are unwilling to do.

When I worked for the VA as legislative program specialist, without fail Congress would always want something delivered to them with little notice and at the worst possible time; late in the day or on a Friday night. My supervisor was a great lady. She always stayed with us, her team, late into the night on many occasions, often providing us with snacks and working by our side, until we completed the task. What I remember most about these late-night episodes was how we bonded like a family, always making sure we had each other's backs. It was unwritten and unspoken among us, but no one left the office for the evening unless we all left together. As the Three Musketeers said, "It is all for one and one for all!"

CHAPTER 7

Principle 5 - Great Leaders Think Creatively

"Never tell people how to do things. Tell them what to do and they will surprise you with their ingenuity."
— George S. Patton Jr., U.S. General

"The visionary starts with a clean sheet of paper, and re-imagines the world."
— Malcolm Gladwell, Author

"If your actions inspire others to dream more, learn more, do more and become more, you are a leader."
— John Quincy Adams, 6th President of the United States

- ▪ *Great leaders think outside the box*

GREAT LEADERS SEEK to approach problems in new and innovative ways, and understand various opinions and solutions in ways that have never occurred to them before.

They look for different sources of inspiration: music, painting, going to the beach, or maybe staring at the stars. I am often most creative when

I am in the horizontal position—lying on the couch or in bed with my eyes closed, visualizing what I'm going to say next, how I'm going to say it, and what the results look like. When my daughter, Alexandria, "Lexy" was about ten years old, I asked her what she was doing on the Internet one day, and she told me she was going to participate in an on-line chat with the author of *The Princess Diaries*, Meg Cabot. My daughter said she was going to ask her some questions, such as "How would you advise someone to get started in writing?" and "How should a young person look for an editor?" I was impressed that Lexy took the initiative to try to learn more about something she loved, writing.

The first thing I wanted to say to her was that there would probably be thousands of people on the online chat trying to get a word in with Meg Cabot. However, I decided to shut-up and let her do her thing because she has been an independent spirit since she was born and I knew she would do it anyway. I left the room, came back about twenty minutes later, and asked her how it was going. She said, "Dad, can you please leave? I'm chatting with Meg Cabot!"

Sure enough, they were messaging each other. I learned a valuable lesson: you should never tell anyone that they can't do something. To this day I have never told my kids they can't do something, the same as you should give your employees the opportunity to innovate and be creative which helps to foster a culture of open and ongoing communication.

- *Great leaders encourage ideas to flicker and promulgate.*

When I was a firefighter in the U.S. Air Force, the term "promulgate" meant that a fire was going to spread if we couldn't contain it. Ideas should become wildfires in our mind's eye and spread so quickly that creativity can flourish. The idea that begets other ideas. There are no mistakes, only ideas, no matter how random they seem. So, how do individuals create the spark that lights the fire?

Ideas need to help solve problems. One tactic is to free your mind from traditional thoughts. Try talking to other people and pick their brains to see how they would do it. Remember, it's not necessary to reinvent the wheel to make it better; just try to make the wheel better. Most people are trapped by starting out too large. Think of the little steps you can take to improve things. For example, can you take a twenty-five-page form and reduce it to five pages for easier use? I encourage you to do something creative and fun. Go for a run, fly a kite, do anything that gives you pleasure. I equate the problem of not being able to problem-solve with the Sudoku puzzles. Often, when I get to the hardest level, and am stuck and can't figure it out, I know it's time to walk away and do something else before trying to solve it again. Strangely enough, when I resume the puzzle, suddenly I'm able to see numbers and patterns I could not previously identify. Finally, what do you know, I'm able to finish the puzzle. The point is that sometimes it takes time, but once the ideas start coming, build on them, and you are off to the races, solving problems. Make sure you follow up once the ideas start flowing by documenting them so you don't forget them.

- ***Great leaders allow others to paint with a blank canvas.***

At one point while working in the federal government, I had a boss tell me I had carte blanche to start a new office to replace an inept organization that was very punitive in nature and dysfunctional. When I asked what he wanted the organization to look like or what his vision for the office was, he said, "That's for you decide. Make it work; that's the reason I hired you! I am giving you the rare opportunity in government—a blank canvas—to create and share your vision of what an organization should look like."

That leader understood that if you hire smart people, get out of their way, and let them do their jobs—surprise! They can do it!

- *Great leaders rely on the innovation of others.*

Steve Jobs said, "Innovation distinguishes between a leader and a follower." Innovation requires the development, production, and implementation of an idea. Therefore, the number of 'latent' innovators are far larger than the number of actual innovations and why we all have, at some point, generated great ideas that we never bothered to implement.

The key difference between creativity and innovation is execution--the capacity to turn an idea into a successful service, product, or venture. If, as William James noted, "Truth is something that happens to an idea," entrepreneurship is the process by which creative ideas become useful innovations.

In my experience the most successful campaigns and initiatives are suggested and developed by employees and fully supported by leadership.

CHAPTER 8

Principle 6 - Great Leaders Communicate Effectively

"Developing excellent communication skills is absolutely essential to effective leadership. The leader must be able to share knowledge and ideas to transmit a sense of urgency and enthusiasm to others. If a leader can't get a message across clearly and motivate others to act on it, then having a message doesn't even matter."
— Gilbert Amelio,
President and CEO of National Semiconductor Corp.

"The basic building block of good communications is the feeling that every human being is unique and of value."
—Unknown

- ***Great leaders powerfully communicate a compelling vision of the future.***

AS JACK WELCH, former Chairman of General Electric said, "Good business leaders create the vision, articulate the vision, passionately own the vision, and relentlessly drive it to completion."

After losing the Democratic primary in New Hampshire in 2016, allies to Hillary Clinton said that her campaign problems boiled down the fact that messages utilizing good character traits and slogans are appropriate but are not a vision. The lesson to be learned in this is that messages and visions need to break out every day to tell people where they are going. They need to be consistent to be effective.

Leaders also need to have clear, well-articulated mission statements to help employees understand the reason for their work.

When I worked for the VA in Washington D.C., it was easy to be inspired, because there isn't an employee of any corporation or business in America, private or public sector, who has a more important and noble mission. The employees who work at the VA Central Office are reminded of this every day when they see the plaque that adorns the front of the building. Pictured at eye-level are the words of Abraham Lincoln, the 16th President of the United States, spoken during his Second Inaugural Address, asking all Americans, "To care for him who shall have borne the battle and for his widow and his orphan." Even in 1865, President Lincoln wrote one of the shortest and perfect mission statements in history for a federal agency that would not begin to exist until 65 years later. Now that is vision!

Let me share my personal mission statement with you. Although a bit lengthy, it clearly defines my reason for existence.

> *I refuse to live a life of mediocrity. I will accomplish excellence in whatever endeavor I choose for my life. I exist to educate, motivate, achieve self-actualization, and become everything that God destined me to be. To become a good husband, father and friend. To champion causes that are important to me. To advocate for those who are less fortunate. To take the time to enjoy the simple joys of*

life. To strive to put the needs of others above my own. To demonstrate wisdom, be humble, and respect the views of others.

Steve Jobs said, "Being the richest man in the cemetery doesn't matter to me. Going to bed at night saying we've done something wonderful, that's what matters to me." Jobs and the other creators of the Apple computer didn't start out building computers just to get rich; they built computers because they loved what they did. They had the vision as Jobs said, "to get a computer in the hands of everyday people, and we succeeded beyond our wildest dreams."

Do you work for a leader who has limited or no vision for the company? Or even worse, a leader who has a vision of his or her own that conflicts with its company and employees?

I worked for the leader of a company who would routinely pump me for information at will, but refused to share what he knew. He never shared his vison of what his company could become, he kept all his plans to himself, isolated other employees from each other and thus his employees lost their respect and in general thought little of him.

My takeaway from this lesson is that leading with vision and being able to see out into the future is compelling, but you must be able to articulate it in a compelling way, too. You must be able to present it and show that there is a plan to help direct and keep people's interest in what they are doing.

- **Great leaders are often charismatic, excitable, and communicate the vision.**

Our Dreams in Action - "Dreams give us hope. Hope ignites passion. Passion leads us to envision success. Visions of success open our minds to recognize opportunity. Recognition of opportunity inspires far-reaching possibilities. Far-reaching possibilities help us enlist support from others. Support from others keeps us focused and committed. Focus and commitment foster action. Action results in progress. Progress leads to achievement. Achievement inspires dreams. Dreams give us hope." –author, Debbie Kennedy.

I always say that hope keeps you from quitting and without hope, we have nothing.

The political pundits were stunned that Donald Trump won the presidency despite no experience as a politician. Why is that? Is it because he says aloud, in plain, blunt, and sometimes crass language, what millions of Americans have long believed, "We're angry because we're run incompetently by incompetent people!" Or is it simply because he wants to "make America great again," because "America's not winning anymore," or because, he says, "We are going to win so much you'll get tired of winning"?

Everyone loves a winner, right? Who can argue with the simplicity of the message? In Bernie Sanders' case, the message was that the top one percent of income earners own America, and we need to make them pay their fair share—equality for all. He tapped into the millennial generation that believes that re-distribution of wealth will make the playing field fair for all. While Donald Trump and Bernie Sanders could not be farther apart ideologically, both built non-traditional movements around their presidential candidacies by appealing to some of the same disaffected voters—those who appreciated blunt talk, alternative facts in Trump's case and delivering an anti-establishment message.

Now contrast that with the signature attack line of the 2016 presidential campaign and label that has stuck, describing former Florida Governor Jeb Bush, "low energy." Ever since Donald Trump used the "low energy" moniker to describe Bush sometime in August

2015, he surged in the polls while the presumed front-runner, Bush, ultimately dropped out of the race. Today, Trump is President of the United States.

- ***Great leaders are transparent and don't leave people waiting for answers.***

A non-responsive boss is just the worst; not responding to people is rude. Real leaders engage with their employees, they return phone calls and emails promptly, and they make themselves available, typically with an open-door policy. Additionally, leaders let their staff know what they are doing while they are working on a project together. They decide who needs to know their schedule, and then they inform those people.

One word we often hear today is "transparency" within organizations. Perhaps one of the best outcomes of such efforts to achieve transparency is the creation of ethically viable organizations that respect their workforce. Transparent leaders do not use deceptive practices, have nothing to hide, and stand proud of the productivity and honest efforts that address their missions. Such organizations don't hide information and keep secrets from key personnel; they foster communication among members and are quick to say thank you. Bad communicators exist everywhere; don't become one of them.

Are you responsive to your family, friends, colleagues and clients? If not, why not? No excuses!

- ***Great leaders inspire others to act.***

The best way to get your team to act is by setting the example. We would be wise to stick to General George Patton's principle of always being willing to do everything you ask of those you command. He also famously said, "We herd sheep, we drive cattle, we lead people. Lead me, follow me, or get out of my way."

Individuals like Patton are relentless, never tiring of restating their visions. They celebrate it, underscore it, put it up in lights everywhere for anyone to see, and make sure that everyone in the organization, from the leader in the corner office to the guy in the mailroom, adheres to it. They adhere to the KISS principle, which is to Keep It Short and Simple or if you prefer - Keep It Simple, Stupid. This ensures a message will be memorable by communicating a clear and simple vision that can be grasped by everyone at every level in the organization. It should be simple enough that it can be passed from one person to the next without distortion or ambiguity. "Great leaders," observes Colin Powell, "are almost always great simplifiers."

Most importantly, though, great leaders inspire others to act by focusing their time and energy on other people. Despite their often busy schedules, they take an active interest in helping workers identify their potential and assisting them in the development of their careers. What's important to them should become what is important to those leading them.

- **Great leaders listen first and value the input of others before speaking.**

"The most basic of all human needs is the need to understand and be understood. The best way to understand people is to listen to them."
— Ralph G. Nichols, Professor Emeritus of Rhetoric,
University of Minnesota

"The most important thing in communication is hearing what isn't said"
— Peter Drucker

Listening is the most overlooked aspect of communication and the hardest to practice for many of us. In full self-disclosure, I have one horrible bad habit, which is interrupting people when they speak. Such a negative character trait! It's not because I'm not listening, it's just that I usually get excited when people are talking. When I know something about the topic, I'm eager to contribute to the conversation. The problem with that, though, is that every time I interrupt someone, it says, "I don't value what you have to have to say."

To stop this bad habit, I was encouraged by a mentor to practice the seven-second rule, which is the polite way of telling me to shut-up for seven seconds before I start speaking. I have apologized numerous times to people for impolitely interrupting them and admitted this is my weakness. To make myself more aware, I have asked staff to hold me accountable by bringing this to my attention when I act out and interrupt others. As leaders, paying attention and being cognizant of people's non-verbal cues is equally important and more telling of what they are actually thinking in a particular moment. When people start yawning, rolling their eyes, tapping the desk, and fidgeting, these are not-so-subtle clues that it might be time for a break before continuing the conversation. Paul Ryan, Speaker of the House of Representatives, had to practice a "poker face" before listening to the 2016 Presidential State of the Union speech.

As leaders, we should resolve to listen better to those around us and to realize this is a skill that must be practiced. Listening well takes commitment. Try to be present in the moment when listening instead of just saying, "Sounds good. Uh-huh," nodding your head, and walking away from the conversation not remembering much of what has been said.

Are you a good listener? Are you present in the moment? Do you provide feedback to your employees to let them know you understand what they have just said?

- ***Great leaders speak with humility that translates into believability.***

I literally humiliated myself and learned the virtue of humility in the process. No matter how smart, successful, good-looking, or special you think you are, nobody likes arrogance and cockiness. It is certainly the quickest way to turn people off.

As a young man in the service, I was nominated for an "Airman of the Quarter" award with another colleague but, to my surprise, he received the award. Instead, of congratulating him, I told our mutual friends that he did not do half of the things he cited in his nomination package. I was angry I did not get the award because I felt like I actually put in the work and deserved the recognition. My colleagues were not impressed that I was not gracious in defeat, and it took a while to gain their confidence back in me as a team player.

I watched Cam Newton, the Carolina Panthers' quarterback, dabbing, styling, and smiling throughout the football season. He did not care if it irked his opponents; he said he was "just being Cam." However, when the Denver Broncos beat his Carolina Panthers in Super Bowl 50, he couldn't run out of the post-game press conference fast enough to avoid the press. Maybe he will learn that a dose of humility is needed to offset a man's ego. Hopefully, because of the loss, he will grow as a leader.

It is important to practice humility to develop into a better leader and person. Humility and vulnerability make us more likable. I have a long way still to go, but each day I remind myself just how small I am in the amazing, wondrous world around me, and that helps me to stay humble. Doing the dishes and taking out the trash help keep my ego in check too; and the time spent with my wife, kids, and dog, who could care less about my work and just want to spend time with me, helps me to keep a proper perspective.

How do you stay humble and authentic to yourself so that it translates into believability?

- ***Great leaders understand everyone has different communication styles.***

Learning to identify the different communication styles – passive, aggressive, manipulative--and recognizing which one we use most often in our daily interactions with friends, family and colleagues, is essential if we want to develop effective, assertive communication skills. Everyone has to be able to tell the difference between the styles, and understand there is a time and place for each one in certain situations.

My personal observation is that women leaders seem more open to allowing for a participatory style of communication by actively discussing problems more openly and utilizing group settings to seek solutions and build consensus. Female leaders typically allow groups to become involved in the decision-making process, thus instilling within the group a sense of ownership of the solution. As a result, the suggestions offered often become more palatable for all employees and easier to incorporate because there is a shared goal. In short, the group members feel their input is valued.

The managerial style of inclusiveness may be attributable to the inherently nurturing role that women are born with or perhaps learn at an early age by observing their mothers taking care of younger or older siblings. Either way, this approach certainly appears to come more naturally for them. Men, on the other hand, tend to communicate in a more authoritative, logical, tough, and formal matter. This format is easier for males because not only are they prepared for the dominant communicative style of an organizational life, but also being male is stereotypically perceived as an integral part of an organization. Men lean on the advice of a few close-knit, trusted advisors for solutions to problems.

I have witnessed fathers telling their young sons not to cry and to toughen up—or else—and have seen the consequences of a son's failed athletic performance. This may help to explain why male leaders are not as accessible, have developed tough exteriors, and make it difficult for their employees to get to know them. I also believe men may not have as open of a communication dialogue style as women because they possibly feel vulnerable or threatened if they expose their true feelings.

The ability to clearly express your thoughts and feelings through open, honest and direct communication is essential to the role of the communicator, regardless of gender.

CHAPTER 9

Principle 7 - Great Leaders Are Agents of Change

"Change is the law of life. And those who look only to the past or present are certain to miss the future."
— John F. Kennedy (1917-1963),
35th President of the U.S.A.

"It is not the strongest of the species that survive, nor the most intelligent, but the one most responsive to change."
— Charles Darwin (1809-1882), English Naturalist

"If you don't like change you'll like irrelevance even less."
— Gen Eric Shinseki,
Secretary of U.S. Department of Veterans Affairs

PRESIDENT OBAMA IN his final state of the union address to a joint session of Congress in 2016, spoke these words about the importance of change:

> We live in a time of extraordinary
> change—change that's reshaping
> the way we live, the way we work,

our planet, and our place in the
world... it's change that promises
amazing medical breakthroughs,
but also economic disruptions that
strain working families. It promises
education for girls in the most remote
villages, but also connects terrorists
plotting an ocean away. It's change
that can broaden opportunity, or
widen inequality. And whether
we like it or not, the pace of the
change will only accelerate. Change
is inevitable; it's a choice of the
consequences we make. I believe in
change because I believe in you.

- ***Great leaders are the change they seek to make.***

As Mahatma Gandhi (1869-1948), the pre-eminent leader of Indian na-
tionalism stated, "You must be the change you wish to see in the world."

Nothing gets accomplished by those sitting on the couch waiting for
things to happen. How many times have you heard people complain
about their elected officials, yet these same people refuse to vote because they say, "It doesn't make any difference," "They are crooked,"
"The system is rigged," and so on. Well, that's the spirit, isn't it?
Hypocrisy doesn't help anything, it can only hurt by laying seeds
for passivity, negativism, laissez-faire attitudes and the deconstruction
of productive possibilities. It's the person who dares to engage who
makes the difference.

I love the quote in President Theodore Roosevelt's April 23, 1910,
speech, "Citizenship in a Republic," in which he talks about the man
in the arena:

It is not the critic who counts, not the
man who points out how the strong
man stumbles, or where the doer of
deeds could have done them better.
The credit belongs to the man who
is actually in the arena, whose face
is marred by dust and sweat and
blood; who strives valiantly; who errs,
who comes short again and again,
because there is no effort without
error and shortcoming; but who
does actually strive to do the deeds;
who knows great enthusiasms, the
great devotions; who spends himself
in a worthy cause; who at the best
knows in the end the triumph of high
achievement, and who at the worst, if
he fails, at least he fails while daring
greatly, so that his place shall never
be with those cold and timid souls
who neither know victory nor defeat.

Say nothing, do nothing, be nothing. Are you a man or woman striving valiantly in that arena?

- *Great leaders don't focus too much time on their critics; they move forward and by virtue of their message their critics convert to believers.*

Great leaders wisely invest their time in the agents of change, and creators of change, rather than focus on their critics.

I want to share a great example of the role of the critic. A critic offers an assessment of arts or culture, food, film and theater, music, your performance at work, and eventually even this book. These reviews typically appear in newspapers, the internet, and social media.

If you've read a critique, especially the day after you've seen the same concert, movie, or play, the critic's impression is often much different than the person who experienced the same event. I often wonder if the critic was actually in the building because they will trash the same event that I just forked over big money to attend. Then it occurred to me, critics feed off of negative criticism. Reading their work can be entertaining, but the purpose and meaning behind their sentiment can be lost with all the negativity. Critics are often judgmental of new talent or creations, but what would the world be without people who create, that share their passion and energy, and ability to inspire others?

In many ways, as workers we become critics when leaders must make changes we may not feel necessary, but are ultimately needed to keep an organization relevant. We come out to resist change, sometimes subtly, sometimes more vociferously, until we come to the realization that the change is needed. Wise leaders move past criticism and negativity and use it as motivation to succeed and get the job done.

As President John F. Kennedy once said, "Change is the law of life, and those who look only to the past or present are certain to miss the future."

- ### *Great leaders don't wait for the Memo.*

Great leaders take action and understand that it is easier to ask forgiveness than permission if they are going to get something done. One of the biggest problems I have observed in twenty-five years of government service is that people are afraid to act out of fear of repercussions. What happens then over time is that employees stagnate, lose creativity and become the very thing they say they would never become when they started their careers: bureaucrats.

A former VA Senior Leader, while addressing my Leadership VA class of 2010, told us that, as leaders, "we should never wait for the Memo." It was his way of saying act, don't stand back and watch things happen, make it happen. This is not something often heard in government service or even large corporations who both seem more interested in keeping the bureaucracy intact rather than meeting the needs of the clients they serve.

One leader I admired was Dr. Gerald Cross, Chief Officer of the Office of Disability and Medical Assessment. He always encouraged me to be creative, welcoming and promoting my ideas to start new programs. He often thanked me (not done often enough by leaders) for being innovative. He never tried to discourage me from being creative, but would instead channel my energy and make me focus to produce manageable and realistic outcomes. He understood the difference between a race horse and a barn horse. As a result, it made me want to do more than just be an average employee; it made me want to be someone who made a difference every day and improved the lives of disabled veterans. It made me eagerly looked forward to going to work each day.

Now, contrast that with an employee who once worked for me. This person would literally stand outside my door each day, asking me the simplest of questions, never taking any initiative to try to figure things out on her own. What made matters worse was that I often had to repeat myself to tell her how to do the things that I had previously shown her numerous times. Yet, this same person was adamant about getting promoted and couldn't understand why she was not getting any jobs with higher responsibility. Similarly, my college-aged daughter, who walks all over her clothes to get to her closet and bathroom, cannot grasp the concept of picking up her room without being told a dozen times. In this instance, I have the leverage of choosing not to help pay for her books, room, meals, car, insurance, etc., until she cleans her room. Withholding or delaying rewards are one way to motivate someone to take initiative and not "wait for the memo".

Making changes within an organization is difficult unless employees are emotionally connected to finding solutions to problems. The ability of leaders to adequately show employees the need for change with a compelling objective they can actually see, touch, and feel, is a powerful, useful mechanism that leaders can use to help an organization embrace change. Such ability also helps motivate employees into taking decisive action. Kotter and Cohen (2002) found that change begins to occur within organizations when leaders compellingly show people what the problems are and how to resolve them. Because of change, the behavior of people—the doubts, fears, and barriers that stifle change are erased, and a climate is created where change can begin to thrive.

Of course, trying to produce behavioral change in just one individual can be challenging, so trying it with a large group of employees and expecting to achieve a specific outcome can produce mixed results.

CHAPTER 10

Principle 8 - Great Leaders Exhibit Confidence

"Trust yourself. Create the kind of self that you will be happy to live with all your life. Make the most of yourself by fanning the tiny, inner sparks of possibility into flames of achievement."

— Golda Meir, 4th Prime Minster of Israel

"But failure has to be an option in art and in exploration— because it's a leap of faith. And no important endeavor that required innovation was done without risk. You have to be willing to take those risks."

— James Cameron, Filmmaker

"People are like stained-glass windows. They sparkle and shine when the sun is out, but when the darkness sets in their true beauty is revealed only if there is light from within."

— Elisabeth Kübler-Ross, Author

- **Great leaders are purposeful and provide their employees with meaningful work.**

MY COLLEGE PROFESSOR, Dr. Thomas Thompson, once told me that "Leaders have the right to require certain actions from employees, but forcing them to do things will only result in getting a sort of mechanical compliance from them. And as leaders, we must understand that people are not static in their existence and experiences; so why would we expect them to be static in their jobs?"

He noted we must also be careful to avoid creating false empowerment. This occurs when leaders appear to invite employees to help find solutions within the organization but then blow off their input or ignore it altogether. As leaders, we need to show caution to not create deception when we have no intention of using any of the employees' suggestions, improvements, or analyses.

Can you see the phoniness of what Dr. Thompson referred to as bogus empowerment? It's not truth-telling or authentic at all.

- ***Great leaders show clarity of thoughts and actions and give others the chance to shine***

Do our words match our actions? Words without actions are meaningless—at least, that is what my wife tells me. The world is full of people who have good intentions, but how many people actually step forward without being prodded by others to follow through. As leaders, we need to step out front but at the same time be cognizant of giving others the opportunity to lead.

This type of leadership was evident in my household without me realizing it. My son, Jeffrey was his high school senior class president and soccer captain. I used to get upset with him because I thought he was leading from behind.

He said, "Dad, I like to give other people the chance to speak and lead, but if I see they can't do it, I'm in the wings ready to make it happen because I already know how to lead." He was not a vocal soccer captain, but rather preferred to let his playing do the talking. He quietly exhorted his younger teammates to step up their play. My son was well-liked by his classmates and teammates without drawing attention to himself. But he always stepped-up when the situation required it.

- ***Great leaders act with a sense of purpose.***

> *"The purpose of life is not to be happy. It is to be useful, to be honorable, to be compassionate, and to have it make some difference that you have lived and lived well."*
> — Ralph Waldo Emerson, American Poet

> *"A life worth living requires that we give of ourselves to others. This requires each of us to find out what motivates us to action in something we believe in."*
> — Richard Leider, Author, *The Power of Purpose*

I have seen the situation numerous times throughout my lifetime: employees do the same job for years and are miserable, working only to make it to retirement and draw their benefits. Generally, I have found that these are the most troublesome employees because they reflect their negativity or unhappiness on others and nothing can be done to make them happy at work. For others, though, especially millennials, they are most likely to quit their jobs not because they don't like their co-workers, leadership, or even pay, but because the work they do is unsatisfying and they see no prospective chances of gaining more meaningful work.

I encourage each of you to follow your passion in finding your life's work, because many of the people whom I respect provide services to others with little pay or fanfare, but can put their heads on their pillows and sleep well at night knowing that they make the world a better place every day.

- ■ *Great leaders show great continence—moderation and self-restraint*

I once worked for a leader who assumed his authoritative leadership style he learned in the military would translate in the real world. Wrong! He verbally tried to beat the hell out of employees to make them submit to his will, and, boy did I feel sorry for those on whom he poured out his wrath with routine tongue-lashings. Berating people illustrates a lack of self-restraint, creates a toxic work environment, and shows that a leader actually feels inferior to his employee, and consequently, feels the need to belittle the employee down to his or her level. Acting maliciously toward others is not how you get people to perform. The old saying that "you will catch more bees with honey" rings true.

The same person above, could have learned from a former co-worker of mine who understood the importance of utilizing soft skills—the personal attributes that enable someone to interact effectively and harmoniously with other people. I saw her repeatedly diffuse many potentially difficult situations by regularly interacting with people and softening her language to make it appropriate and tailored for each circumstance and person.

Good manners, optimism, common sense, a sense of humor, empathy, and the ability to collaborate and negotiate are all important soft skills. Other soft skills include situational awareness, and the ability to read a situation as it unfolds to decide on a response that yields the best results for all involved.

Another important soft skill is adaptability. An employee with this attribute can work in various situations equally well and move from one situation to another with ease and grace. The ability to be diplomatic and respectful even when there are disagreements is also a key soft skill. This skill requires leaders and employees alike to maintain a professional tone and demeanor even when frustrated.

CHAPTER **11**

Principle 9 - Great Leaders Are Capable

"What we can or cannot do, what we consider possible or impossible, is rarely a function of our true capability. It is more likely a function of our beliefs about who we are."

— Anthony Robbins,
Author and Motivational Speaker

"Most of life's actions are within our reach, but decisions take willpower."
— Robert McKee, *Story: Style, Structure, Substance, and the Principles of Screenwriting*

"One is not a genuine leader if one does not foster capable successors. True success cannot be achieved without fostering talented individuals and nurturing their potential."

— Buddhist philosopher

▪ ***Great leaders show technical competence.***

TECHNICAL COMPETENCE IS an effective application of a skill, and something that can be learned. Great leaders should still retain technical competence even in duties they no longer are required to perform regularly.

The Chinese axiom or biblical principle "Give a man a fish, and you have fed him once. Teach him how to fish and you have fed him for a lifetime," is important because your employees and even your own children will come to you eager to learn a new skill or to show how they can perform a task. Rarely will you find a person who will be technically competent from day one. Those working for you will have to rely on you to guide them and show them the way, so it is important that you retain technical competency.

I remember my first day on the job at my first assignment as an Air Force firefighter. I was scared to death. Some thirty-five-year-old supervisor came up to me as I was trying to load a hose onto the fire truck and asked why it was taking so long. I explained that I was loading the hose the way I was taught to in fire school but that it wasn't working. He laughed and said, *"Forget everything you learned. I'm going to show you the way we do it in the real world."*

As your career advances, at some point, you will be promoted to a job that demands responsibility for areas outside your specialty. Your colleagues will ask questions that you cannot answer and may not even understand. You may ask yourself, how can I lead these tech savvy millennials who know more about their work than I do?

One of the first things we need to recognize as leaders is to know no one knows it all, acknowledge your limitations and seek help or guidance from the people who know how to get the job done. Admitting that you don't know everything doesn't make you less of a leader. In fact, your colleagues will find it a breath of fresh air that you come to count on them for technical expertise.

- **Great leaders make distinctions between the person and the employee.**

Throughout my career, I have had a number of employees who were average at accomplishing their tasks and who were content just to punch a clock and be the first ones out the door at the end of the day. I once wanted to promote a very educated woman, an attorney, to a higher level of responsibility and pay, but she flat out told me, *"I don't want the responsibility. I just want to do my job and go home at the end of the day. It's not worth listening to other people's problems."* I think an important thing we, as leaders, need to remember is that we must keep our egocentrism in check. The traditional definition of egocentrism is an inability to understand or assume any perspective other than our own.

The problem is that when we incorporate our personal beliefs about the world, we can invoke both positive and negative judgments of others and believe that our way is the only way. We must also guard against the proverbial halo effect, which means just because one employee is great at a particular task, we cannot automatically assume he or she is great at everything. Even if an employee has erred on a task or assignment, one can critique the situation and still let that person keep their dignity.

Our goal as leaders should be to invest our time and energy in the people with whom we work and serve. Based on my experience, I believe that leaders should aim to leave businesses better than when they first started, show concern for their employees, and create stronger family bonds that ultimately transform the world for the better. I also think when we meet with people in private settings to discuss their performance, they should leave our office with a clear understanding of our concern for them as employees and as individuals, and walk away with more pride in knowing that we value their contributions to the company.

The fact is, though, that the practical and applied realities of working with others require certain compromises. Understand that at times, your ethical practices and personal values will be tested, but the job as a leader does not require that those ethics and values be subject to situational determinants of change. Think of these realities of compromise as a way to expand your perspectives to allow for differences in opinion, experiences, beliefs, and representational duties.

Another way to interpret what I'm trying to say is that the ability to deeply understand how people can so differ from one another in all facets of their lives is important. Though they may differ from what we are familiar with or might expect—they are what they are, and finding ways to communicate in a respectful, pleasant, and civilized manner is far more challenging and far more desirable than reducing ourselves.

It is also beneficial to realize that people differ vastly in the views of their lives. With this realization we are able to open our understanding of how people behave and think, so much so, that it may lead us to a higher order of acceptance and empathy.

- ***Great leaders are not afraid to seek the advice and counsel of others***

Leaders who know what they don't know are smart enough to learn from others who have more experience. They are not afraid to let someone know that they don't have all the answers. Who does? Even so-called experts are not always right—take weather forecasters and politicians for example—but they must be willing to find out the answers to maintain their credibility and influence.

Those who don't know, wisely seek counsel from someone who's more familiar with the situation at hand, because the best advice often comes from others who have personally faced similar circumstances, even if the advice is "Don't do what I did."

When I was a young airman, I was named "Airman of the Year" for 1003rd Civilian Engineering Squadron at Peterson AFB, in Colorado Springs, Colorado. I was then sent to compete for Airman of the Year for the entire base. As I sat before the review board, I was pretty polished and thought I had a good chance of winning. I provided clear, articulate answers to the first three questions. No problem, I thought, I got this.

But then came the dreaded final question that to this day I'll never forget. I was asked to describe something that had to do with service accoutrements. I had no idea what the hell they were talking about, so I politely asked if I could sit there in silence to think about it. In my mind, I was thinking, *Shit! I'm toast!* I proceeded to rattle off the most rambling response I have ever given in my entire life. Everyone in the room was staring at me as I tried to bluff my way through the answer. I can still see them sitting there dazed, trying not to laugh. I knew right there and then that I was done—I blew my big chance.

After the interview, I spoke with another nominee in the hallway and asked him what the hell an accoutrement was. He said, "I have no idea."

I asked him, "How did you respond to the question?"

He replied, "I told them I didn't know the answer, and we moved on and finished the interview." That's it, I thought. Such a simple solution because it was the most obvious. I was trying to impress everyone, but instead embarrassed myself in the process. Lesson learned. Stay humble, be coachable, seek and learn from others, and don't be afraid to tell them what you don't know.

Do you know what you don't know? And do you seek advice from counsel and others?

- ***Great leaders build relationships or else lose the confidence of the employees in their ability to lead.***

Leaders must always be willing to intervene and know where trouble lurks. One useful tactic is to sit in on a meeting between two individuals to see if the conversation flows back and forth between the two parties. If it does that's a good sign. If the leader does all the talking and the subordinates are passive, that's a bad sign, and you can conclude that you need to dig more deeply. Notice that you don't need any expertise on the subject they are discussing; you just need to decide if the conversation is healthy.

Great leaders schedule discussions with their employees to provide clarity and help them meet the upcoming challenges. You cannot expect employees to perform without knowing what the standards are and then provide them with an assessment where they have no idea on how they will be evaluated until after the fact. It is not fair to expect them to read your mind.

When leaders fail to build successful relationships, employees begin to see them as inept, incapable of leading, and unconcerned with the value that the employee brings to the organization.

CHAPTER 13

Principle 10 - Great Leaders Show Character

"Nearly all men can stand adversity, but if you want to test a man's character, give him power."
— Abraham Lincoln, 16th President of the United States

"Always do right. It will gratify some people and astonish the rest."
— Mark Twain, American author and humorist

- ***Great leaders exhibit ethical strength.***

ST. AUGUSTINE FAMOUSLY said, "If I said it, I must believe it; if I did it, I must think it is right."

The issue of "ethical" self-deception is perhaps the key to distinguishing between leaders who are consistently ethical and those who find themselves (sometimes unconsciously) behaving inappropriately. In David Luban's *Moral Leadership: The Theory and Practice of Power, Judgment and Policy*, he notes, "When our conduct clashes with our prior beliefs, our beliefs swing into conformity with our conduct, without our noticing that it is going on."

How many times have you heard politicians who rail against the fossil fuel industry and big banks and then turn around and accept campaign money from the same organizations? Does this seem ethical? I believe they try to compartmentalize their words to justify taking their funds. It can be off-putting when we find people in our lives who seem absolutely committed to their opinions and beliefs and seem judgmental when people disagree with them. Part of becoming educated and mature is the acceptance of the differences among people.

Dr. Thomas Thompson, from Nova Southeastern University says,

> We all have people in the workplace who make us crazy; and I advise most people to have a screaming pillow at home or in their office into which we can just scream our lungs out to vent, or meditate, do yoga, or go for a swim, or listen to music—but don't kick the dog when you get home. We do need to pick our hills to die on. Do know that discourteous acts and cowardly acts of blame are transparent to most of us at work. That is, our "humanity" and abilities to empathize and read character in people is accurate. Those people who don't have the strength of character or courage to admit strengths or incompetence will likely fail in the long term.

- ***Great leaders are willing to fall on the sword for their ethical beliefs.***

The most powerful example I have seen regarding an example of following one's ethical belief occurred when I worked for the Veterans Health Administration. Dr. Michael Kussman, the Undersecretary for Health was summoned to appear before the Senate Committee on Veterans' Affairs staff to discuss a contentious union issue involving mandatory healthcare training/patient care. The union leadership pushed back on the need to require this training and was trying to dictate healthcare policy. Before we even left VA Central Office to head to the Hill, Dr. Kussman told everyone traveling with him that if the Senate did not bacz him on this issue, he would resign that day from the Veterans Health Administration. I was stunned, because I finally found a leader who was willing to do the right thing–to fall on the sword for his beliefs! That took courage! Thankfully, Dr. Kussman prevailed.

Individuals who understand the components of ethical decision-making and who can objectively view a situation and apply ethical principles will likely make decisions consistent with their true beliefs and intentions.

Another well-publicized, albeit some would consider political stunt event, involved a Kentucky county clerk, Kim Davis, who refused to issue same-sex marriage certificates. She suspended issuing marriage licenses from her office so everyone would be treated the same, stating plainly her objections to being forced by the state to violate her faith. My personal feeling is that she had a duty as an elected public servant to uphold her oath and issue the certificates regardless of her beliefs. However, she believed it was against her personal moral compass and was willing to go to jail for her beliefs. At least she got to meet the Pope when he visited the United States (not that the Archdiocese was happy about it). Right or wrong, how many people do you know who would stand ready to go jail for their ethical beliefs?

- **Great leaders show moral courage.**

Character counts! Leaders always have choices. Moral courage means doing the right thing, even at the risk of inconvenience, ridicule, punishment, and the loss of a job, security, or social status. Moral courage requires that we rise above the apathy, complacency, hatred, cynicism, and fear-mongering in our political systems, socio-economic divisions, and cultural and religious differences.

In the workplace, moral courage is the willingness to confront a situation for the sake of rightness, independent of the cost. Examples of moral courage in the workplace include telling a supervisor about how your co-workers frequently doctor their timesheets, disclosing illegal accounting practices to an external auditor, or releasing incriminating confidential documents to the media. Disclosure of illicit or unsavory business practices to the public is also known as "whistleblowing." This is another form of moral courage.

Benefits of moral courage may include improving or transforming corporate culture, creating a more equitable workplace, and helping better society. By the exposure of injustices in the office, the responsible parties should hopefully change their ways.

- *Great leaders act in good faith.*

I once had an individual tell me that he did not trust anyone in business. I literally almost dropped the phone, because this runs counter to everything I believe. I always try to see the best in people and consider everyone to be a top employee/person unless they prove otherwise. From that moment on, I listened skeptically to everything he said because I believe if you think that of others, it's likely that you are the one that cannot be trusted.

One example of acting in good faith would be when baseball teams trade players. The intent is for each team to get the maximum value or best deal it can for the players it thinks can help the team win. The goal for both parties is to create a win-win-win situation in which both parties can walk away knowing the deal they made from a player or financial standpoint is beneficial to everyone involved.

To create a win-win-win situation (I win, you win, and we both win only when we work together) requires that both parties act in good faith and that they both engage in open, honest, and clear communication. Questions, explanations, and answers should be provided that address the needs, wishes, and expectations of all involved. Listen carefully to what is being said and by whom it is being said, and then make an informed decision.

- **Great leaders try to find common interests.**

When my son was growing up, I had a difficult time for a few years trying to understand him. He is much more like my wife: quiet, private, analytic and reflective. He did not like playing or even trying to play the same sports (baseball, basketball, football) that I grew-up watching. He loved and developed a passion for playing soccer, but I knew nothing about the game and, frankly, didn't care much for it. However, by chance, someone needed to step-up and coach his youth teams. I soon learned to appreciate and enjoy something that he liked, remember it's not always about us, and thus it bonded us together. When I could no longer coach him at a higher level, and make his practices due to work commitments, it bothered me that we no longer got to spend this special time together. Now, that my son is away at Florida State attending college, I would give everything to go back in time, to coach and watch him play soccer again--tears.

As a leader, there will be many times throughout your career and life when you must sacrifice and learn to do things that other people enjoy doing if you are to make a situation work—just like in a marriage. One way to find commonalities with people is to start with the general things you might have in common, such as — "Hey, we both like food!" —and work your way to more specific things — "Wow, we both love pizza!" You will soon find out that more people than not share common interests with you.

Have you ever watched the U.S. president give a speech and observe how, before he even finishes, the opposition party is already attacking and condemning the speech? Or have you seen how when President Obama was elected and the minority leader's first words are about making him a one-term president? The point is that leaders of character must display a long-term commitment that requires hard work, a willingness to face up to difficult problems, and an ability to display humility and be pleasant even when things get tough, says John Mertz, "we need to remember to be big in our character and small in our personality."

The pressure for CEOs, employers, managers, and leaders to deliver and produce income and results is overwhelming. It is precisely this type of pressure that leads individuals to engage in behavior that compromises their ethical principles.

Final Chapter

HERE ARE MY final musings that I hope will inspire my reader friends.

Today is the first day of the rest of your life. How will you finish the sentence? What will your life count for? Albert Pike once said, "What we have done for ourselves alone dies with us; what we have done for others and the world remains and is forever." How will you be remembered by those who love you, by those who have worked with and for you? Did you live a life that you are proud of? Was it in service to others? Looking into the future, what does your legacy statement look like?

Here's mine:

> *He was full of life and energy and used his gifts and strengths to make wise decisions and to have a more positive, beneficial, and sustainable impact on others.*

> *His purpose in life was to serve others. He strived to live a life of integrity and be a role model to others.*

> *He loved his wife and children more than words could express and was incredibly blessed with their love that made his life more fulfilling and meaningful.*

It has been a privilege writing this book, and it has energized me to share these ideas, because, for me, the end has always been about the journey, and the journey had to start somewhere. The journey for me was to fulfill a promise to myself, which was to complete this book. Mission accomplished!

We all find ourselves in emotional struggles, but if we can take some time for reflection, I think we will find it to be a very good way to help ourselves, as we need to make rational, competent, and informed decisions. I hope you will use these **10 "C "Leadership Principles** as reminders and as thinking strategies to employ your ethical commitments to the people with whom you love and work.

Remember, a good leader is like a steady point guard on a basketball team. He may not be the superstar player who can hit the impossible, game-winning shots—a lá a Michael Jordan or Kobe Bryant—or make a spectacular slam dunk that drives the crowd into a frenzy. But the point guard controls the game, sets the tempo at which the team plays, collects and calms team members down when the other team is rallying, moves people into the right positions to get the ball, and delivers the pass to team members at exactly the right moments to allow the team to score. And on defense, the point guard plays at the top of the key, disrupts anticipating plays, and sacrifices his or her body to take a charge for the team. The point guard doesn't care if he or she scores and doesn't look at the box score after the game to see his or her statistics. The point guard is concerned with only two things: getting the team involved and winning the game.

My favorite basketball player of all time is Earvin "Magic" Johnson, formerly of the Los Angeles Lakers. In watching a 22-minute compilation of his career highlights on YouTube, one thing that stood out to me was that the video did not show him take a single shot until the 7th minute in the clip. I found this quite remarkable, because, indeed, to this day, nearly two decades since his retirement, Magic is universally regarded as one of the greatest players to ever play the game because of his unique ability to get others involved in the game and his outstanding leadership qualities that willed his teammates to victory. Every workplace needs a point guard to steady the team.

Jerry Smith, who played tight end for the Washington Redskins football team from 1965 – 1977, when he was on his deathbed said this about the legendary Green Bay Packers coach, Vince Lombardi: "Every important thing a man searches for in his life, I found in Coach Lombardi. He made us men. A football player is like a wheel, and every spoke is very important to the balance of the wheel--team. Continue, just continue. Try to be great athletes, but don't forget to be great friends, teammates above all, and leaders."

> Be authentic and good luck in all you do, because you can do it!
>
> — Jeff

Acknowledgements

Writing this book would not have been possible without the support of my wife, my rock, Tammy; two kids, Jeffrey and Lexy; and my most ardent follower who sat with me as I typed every word, my golden retriever, Shelby.

I want to thank my former professor at Nova Southeastern University, Dr. Thomas J. Thompson, for getting me to think about leadership in a more memorable way. His well-thought-out comments and interactions with me and my classmates were exemplary and inspired me, in part, to write this book.

I also want to thank my many former colleagues and supervisors for sharing their stories about the poor leadership they endured and had to overcome just to do their jobs effectively. Despite the many crazy leadership stories that I've heard and personally endured, it has been an encouragement for me to see the human spirit overcome through the commitment of outstanding employees dedicated to contributing in the workplace, despite their challenges with mediocre leaders.

For everyone else who has known or interacted with me over the years, thanks for your patience with me, and, most importantly, for believing in me despite my many shortcomings. Your trust in me over the years led me to believe that I had something to offer that needed to be said. I hope my words of encouragement and stories that I've shared will resonate and inspire others to practice **The 10 "C" Leadership Principles of Excellence**.

References

Baldoni, J, Dean Smith Coaching Us To Do The Right Thing. Forbes. February 8, 2015. http://www.forbes.com/sites/johnbaldoni/2015/02/08/dean-smith-coaching-us-to-do-the-right-thing/#182e709c5f7c

Steve Harvey Show. Harvey's Hero: Mark Pizzo. Feb 10, 2016. http://www.steveharveytv.com/harveys-hero-mark-pizzo/ vivo

Bird, B. *Ratatouille*. Hollywood, California: Walt Disney Company, 2007, DVD.

Dr. Thompson, T, Nova Southeastern University, Weekly Discussion Topic, October 16, 2008, Retrieved electronically from WebCT Discussion Board 10/08.

Mertz, J. "What Builds Character?" January 9, 2016. https://www.thindifference.com/2016/01/what-builds-character/

Luban D. *Moral leadership: The Theory and Practice of Power, Judgment, and Policy*. San Francisco, CA: Jossey-Bass, 2006.

Callahan, T. "He Was One of Us." *Sport Illustrated*, January 11, 2016, 59-65.

About the Author

Jeff Scarpiello is a medically retired service-disabled veteran with over twenty years of veterans' advocacy, policy, and strategic planning experience. He has worked for two national veteran non-profits, the federal and legislative branches of government, and in the corporate business sector.

Jeff earned his bachelor of arts from Excelsior College in New York (cum laude, 2001) and earned his Master of Science in Leadership at Nova Southeastern University, in 2012. Jeff is a graduate of Leadership VA, class of 2010, and served as class president. He was selected into the prestigious Partnership for Public Service Excellence in Government Fellows Program in 2013.

He is a recipient of the Partnership for Public Service - 2015 Citizen in Action Award for a homeless pilot project initiative leveraging partnerships to help cover move-in costs for homeless veterans, helping to make their houses homes.

He enjoys spending time with his wife, Tammy; children, Jeffrey and Alexandria "Lexy" and dog, Shelby. He enjoys cooking and travelling, especially taking cruises to feel the ocean breeze.

CPSIA information can be obtained
at www.ICGtesting.com
Printed in the USA
FFOW03n0433210817
39056FF

9 781478 784586